JAMESTOWN

Timed Readings Plus *in Science*

25 Two-Part Lessons
with Questions for
Building Reading Speed and Comprehension

BOOK 7

Glencoe McGraw-Hill

New York, New York   Columbus, Ohio   Chicago, Illinois   Peoria, Illinois   Woodland Hills, California

JAMESTOWN EDUCATION

Glencoe/McGraw-Hill

A Division of The McGraw·Hill Companies

ISBN: 0-07-827376-5

Send all queries to:
Glencoe/McGraw-Hill
8787 Orion Place
Columbus, OH 43240-4027

5 6 7 8 9 10 021 08

CONTENTS

You probably talk at an average rate of about 150 words a minute. If you are a reader of average ability, you read at a rate of about 250 words a minute. So your reading speed is nearly twice as fast as your speaking or listening speed. This example shows that reading is one of the fastest ways to get information.

The purpose of this book is to help you increase your reading rate and understand what you read. The 25 lessons in this book will also give you practice in reading science articles and in preparing for tests in which you must read and understand nonfiction passages within a certain time limit.

Reading Faster and Better

Following are some strategies that you can use to read the articles in each lesson.

Previewing

Previewing before you read is a very important step. This helps you to get an idea of what a selection is about and to recall any previous knowledge you have about the subject. Here are the steps to follow when previewing.

Read the title. Titles are designed not only to announce the subject but also to make the reader think. Ask yourself questions such as What can I learn from the title? What thoughts does it bring to mind?

What do I already know about this subject?

Read the first sentence. If they are short, read the first two sentences. The opening sentence is the writer's opportunity to get your attention. Some writers announce what they hope to tell you in the selection. Some writers state their purpose for writing; others just try to get your attention.

Read the last sentence. If it is short, read the final two sentences. The closing sentence is the writer's last chance to get ideas across to you. Some writers repeat the main idea once more. Some writers draw a conclusion—this is what they have been leading up to. Other writers summarize their thoughts; they tie all the facts together.

Skim the entire selection. Glance through the selection quickly to see what other information you can pick up. Look for anything that will help you read fluently and with under-standing. Are there names, dates, or numbers? If so, you may have to read more slowly.

Reading for Meaning

Here are some ways to make sure you are making sense of what you read.

Build your concentration. You cannot understand what you read if you are not concentrating. When you discover that your thoughts are straying, correct the situation right away. Avoid distractions and distracting situations. Keep in mind the information you learned from previewing. This will help focus your attention on the selection.

Read in thought groups. Try to see meaningful combinations of words—phrases, clauses, or sentences. If you look at only one word at a time (called word-by-word reading), both your comprehension and your reading speed suffer.

Ask yourself questions. To sustain the pace you have set for yourself and to maintain a high level of concentration and comprehension, ask yourself questions such as What does this mean? or How can I use this information? as you read.

Finding the Main Ideas

The paragraph is the basic unit of meaning. If you can quickly discover and understand the main idea of each paragraph, you will build your comprehension of the selection.

Find the topic sentence. The topic sentence, which contains the main idea, often is the first sentence of a paragraph. It is followed by sentences that support, develop, or explain the main idea. Sometimes a topic sentence comes at the end of a paragraph. When it does, the supporting details come first, building the base for the topic sentence. Some paragraphs do not have a topic sentence; all of the sentences combine to create a meaningful idea.

Understand paragraph structure. Every well-written paragraph has a purpose. The purpose may be to inform, define, explain or illustrate. The purpose should always relate to the main idea and expand on it. As you read each paragraph, see how the body of the paragraph tells you more about the main idea.

Relate ideas as you read. As you read the selection, notice how the writer puts together ideas. As you discover the relationship between the ideas, the main ideas come through quickly and clearly.

Mastering Reading Comprehension

Reading fast is not useful if you don't remember or understand what you read. The two exercises in Part A provide a check on how well you have understood the article.

Recalling Facts

These multiple-choice questions provide a quick check to see how well you recall important information from the article. As you learn to apply the reading strategies described earlier, you should be able to answer these questions more successfully.

Understanding Ideas

These questions require you to think about the main ideas in the article. Some main ideas are stated in the article; others are not. To answer some of the questions, you need to draw conclusions about what you read.

The five exercises in Part B require multiple answers. These exercises provide practice in applying comprehension and critical-thinking skills that you can use in all your reading.

Recognizing Words in Context

Always check to see whether the words around an unfamiliar word—its context—can give you a clue to the word's meaning. A word generally appears in a context related to its meaning.

Suppose, for example, that you are unsure of the meaning of the word *expired* in the following passage:

> Vera wanted to check out a book, but her library card had expired. She had to borrow my card, because she didn't have time to renew hers.

You could begin to figure out the meaning of *expired* by asking yourself a question such as, What could have happened to Vera's library card that would make her need to borrow someone else's card? You might realize that if Vera had to renew her card, its usefulness must have come to an end or run out. This would lead you to conclude that the word *expired* must mean "to come to an end" or "to run out." You would be right. The context suggested the meaning.

Context can also affect the meaning of a word you already know. The word *key,* for instance, has many meanings. There are musical keys, door keys, and keys to solving a mystery. The context in which the word *key* occurs will tell you which meaning is correct.

Sometimes a word is explained by the words that immediately follow it. The subject of a sentence and your knowledge about that subject might also help you determine the meaning of an unknown word. Try to decide the meaning of the word *revive* in the following sentence:

> Sunshine and water will revive those drooping plants.

The compound subject is *sunshine* and *water*. You know that plants need light and water to survive and that drooping plants are not healthy. You can figure out that *revive* means "to bring back to health."

Distinguishing Fact from Opinion

Every day you are called upon to sort out fact and opinion. Because much of what you read and hear contains both facts and opinions, you need to be able to tell the two apart.

Facts are statements that can be proved true. The proof must be objective and verifiable. You must be able to check for yourself to confirm a fact.

Look at the following facts. Notice that they can be checked for accuracy and confirmed. Suggested sources for verification appear in parentheses.

- Abraham Lincoln was the 16th president of the United States. (Consult biographies, social studies books, encyclopedias, and similar sources.)

- Earth revolves around the Sun. (Research in encyclopedias or astronomy books; ask knowledgeable people.)

- Dogs walk on four legs. (See for yourself.)

Opinions are statements that cannot be proved true. There is no objective evidence you can consult to check the truthfulness of an opinion. Unlike facts, opinions express personal beliefs or judgments. Opinions reveal how someone feels about a subject, not the facts about that subject. You might agree or disagree with someone's opinion, but you cannot prove it right or wrong.

Look at the following opinions. The reasons these statements are classified as opinions appear in parentheses.

- Abraham Lincoln was born to be a president. (You cannot prove this by referring to birth records. There is no evidence to support this belief.)

- Earth is the only planet in our solar system where intelligent life exists. (There is no proof of this. It may be proved true some day, but for now it is just an educated guess—not a fact.)

- The dog is a human's best friend. (This is not a fact; your best friend might not be a dog.)

As you read, be aware that facts and opinions are often mixed together. Both are useful to you as a reader. But to evaluate what you read and to read intelligently, you need to know the difference between the two.

Keeping Events in Order

Sequence, or chronological order, is the order of events in a story or article or the order of steps in a process. Paying attention to the sequence of events or steps will help you follow what is happening, predict what might happen next, and make sense of a passage.

To make the sequence as clear as possible, writers often use signal words to help the reader get a more exact idea of when things happen. Following is a list of frequently used signal words and phrases:

until	first
next	then
before	after
finally	later
when	while
during	now
at the end	by the time
as soon as	in the beginning

Signal words and phrases are also useful when a writer chooses to relate details or events out of sequence. You need to pay careful attention to determine the correct chronological order.

Making Correct Inferences

Much of what you read *suggests* more than it *says*. Writers often do not state ideas directly in a text. They can't. Think of the time and space it would take to state every idea. And think of how boring that would be! Instead, writers leave it to you, the reader, to fill in the information they leave out—to make inferences. You do this by combining clues in the story or article with knowledge from your own experience.

You make many inferences every day. Suppose, for example, that you are visiting a friend's house for the first time. You see a bag of kitty litter. You infer (make an inference) that the family has a cat. Another day you overhear a conversation. You catch the names of two actors and the words *scene, dialogue,* and *directing.* You infer that the people are discussing a movie or play.

In these situations and others like them, you infer unstated information from what you observe or read. Readers must make inferences in order to understand text.

Be careful about the inferences you make. One set of facts may suggest several inferences. Some of these inferences could be faulty. A correct inference must be supported by evidence.

Remember that bag of kitty litter that caused you to infer that your friend has a cat? That could be a faulty inference. Perhaps your friend's family uses the kitty litter on their icy sidewalks to create traction. To be sure your inference is correct, you need more evidence.

Understanding Main Ideas

The main idea is the most important idea in a paragraph or passage—the idea that provides purpose and direction. The rest of the selection explains, develops, or supports the main idea. Without a main idea, there would be only a collection of unconnected thoughts.

In the following paragraph, the main idea is printed in italics. As you read, observe how the other sentences develop or explain the main idea.

Typhoon Chris hit with full fury today on the central coast of Japan. Heavy rain from the storm flooded the area. High waves carried many homes into the sea. People now fear that the heavy rains will cause mudslides in the central part of the country. The number of people killed by the storm may climb past the 200 mark by Saturday.

In this paragraph, the main-idea statement appears first. It is followed by sentences that explain, support, or give details. Sometimes the main idea appears at the end of a paragraph. Writers often put the main idea at the end of a paragraph when their purpose is to persuade or convince. Readers may be more open to a new idea if the reasons for it are presented first.

As you read the following paragraph, think about the overall impact of the supporting ideas. Their purpose is to convince the reader that the main idea in the last sentence should be accepted.

Last week there was a head-on collision at Huntington and Canton streets. Just a month ago a pedestrian was struck there. Fortunately, she was only slightly injured. In the past year, there have been more accidents there than at any other corner in the city. In fact, nearly 10 percent of all accidents in the city occur at the corner. This intersection is very dangerous, and a traffic signal should be installed there before a life is lost.

The details in the paragraph progress from least important to most important. They achieve their full effect in the main idea statement at the end.

In many cases, the main idea is not expressed in a single sentence. The reader is called upon to interpret all of the ideas expressed in the paragraph and to decide upon a main idea. Read the following paragraph.

> The American author Jack London was once a pupil at the Cole Grammar School in Oakland, California. Each morning the class sang a song. When the teacher noticed that Jack wouldn't sing, she sent him to the principal. He returned to class with a note. The note said that Jack could be excused from singing with the class if he would write an essay every morning.

In this paragraph, the reader has to interpret the individual ideas and to decide on a main idea. This main idea seems reasonable: Jack London's career as a writer began with a punishment in grammar school.

Understanding the concept of the main idea and knowing how to find it is important. Transferring that understanding to your reading and study is also important.

Working Through a Lesson

Part A

1. **Preview the article.** Locate the timed selection in Part A of the lesson that you are going to read. Wait for your teacher's signal to preview. You will have 20 seconds for previewing. Follow the previewing steps described on page 2.

2. **Read the article.** When your teacher gives you the signal, begin reading. Read carefully so that you will be able to answer questions about what you have read. When you finish reading, look at the board and note your reading time. Write this time at the bottom of the page on the line labeled Reading Time.

3. **Complete the exercises.** Answer the 10 questions that follow the article. There are 5 fact questions and 5 idea questions. Choose the best answer to each question and put an X in that box.

4. **Correct your work.** Use the Answer Key at the back of the book to check your answers. Circle any wrong answer and put an X in the box you should have marked. Record the number of correct answers on the appropriate line at the end of the lesson.

Part B

1. **Preview and read the passage.** Use the same techniques you

used to read Part A. Think about what you are reading.

2. **Complete the exercises.** Instructions are given for answering each category of question. There are 15 responses for you to record.

3. **Correct your work.** Use the Answer Key at the back of the book. Circle any wrong answer and write the correct letter or number next to it. Record the number of correct answers on the appropriate line at the end of the lesson.

Plotting Your Progress

1. **Find your reading rate.** Turn to the Reading Rate graph on page 116. Put an X at the point where the vertical line that represents the lesson intersects your reading time, shown along the left-hand side. The right-hand side of the graph will reveal your words-per-minute reading speed.

2. **Find your comprehension score.** Add your scores for Part A and Part B to determine your total number of correct answers. Turn to the Comprehension Score graph on page 117. Put an X at the point where the vertical line that represents your lesson intersects your total correct answers, shown along the left-hand side. The right-hand side of the graph will show the percentage of questions you answered correctly.

3. **Complete the Comprehension Skills Profile.** Turn to page 118. Record your incorrect answers for the Part B exercises. The five Part B skills are listed along the bottom. There are five columns of boxes, one column for each question. For every incorrect answer, put an X in a box for that skill.

To get the most benefit from these lessons, you need to take charge of your own progress in improving your reading speed and comprehension. Studying these graphs will help you to see whether your reading rate is increasing and to determine what skills you need to work on. Your teacher will also review the graphs to check your progress.

About the Series

Timed Readings Plus in Science includes 10 books at reading levels 4–13, with one book at each level. Book One contains material at a fourth-grade reading level; Book Two at a fifth-grade level, and so on. The readability level is determined by the Fry Readability Scale and is not to be confused with grade or age level. The books are designed for use with students at middle-school level and above.

The purposes of the series are as follows:

- to provide systematic, structured reading practice that helps students improve their reading rate and comprehension skills

- to give students practice in reading and understanding informational articles in the content area of science

- to give students experience in reading various text types—informational, expository, narrative, and prescriptive

- to prepare students for taking standardized tests that include timed reading passages in various content areas

- to provide materials with a wide range of reading levels so that students can continue to practice and improve their reading rate and comprehension skills

Because the books are designed for use with students at designated reading levels rather than in a particular grade, the science topics in this series are not correlated to any grade-level curriculum. Most standardized tests require students to read and comprehend science passages. This series provides an opportunity for students to become familiar with the particular requirements of reading science. For example, the vocabulary in a science article is important. Students need to know certain words in order to understand the concepts and the information.

Each book in the series contains 25 two-part lessons. Part A focuses on improving reading rate. This section of the lesson consists of a 400-word timed informational article on a science topic followed by two multiple-choice exercises. Recalling Facts includes five fact questions; Understanding Ideas includes five critical-thinking questions.

Part B concentrates on building mastery in critical areas of comprehension. This section consists of a nontimed passage—the "plus" passage—followed by five exercises that address five major comprehension skills. The passage varies in length; its subject matter relates to the content of the timed selection.

Timed Reading and Comprehension

Timed reading is the best-known method of improving reading speed. There is no point in someone's reading at an accelerated speed if the person does not understand what she or he is reading. Nothing is more important than comprehension in reading. The main purpose of reading is to gain knowledge and insight, to understand the information that the writer and the text are communicating.

Few students will be able to read a passage once and answer all of the questions correctly. A score of 70 or 80 percent correct is normal. If the student gets 90 or 100 percent correct, he or she is either reading too slowly or the material is at too low a reading level. A comprehension or critical thinking score of less than 70 percent indicates a need for improvement.

One method of improving comprehension and critical-thinking skills is for the student to go back and study each incorrect answer. First, the student should reread the question carefully. It is surprising how many students get the wrong answer simply because they have not read the question carefully. Then the student should look back in the passage to find the place where the question is answered, reread that part of the passage, and think about how to arrive at the correct answer. It is important to be able to recognize a correct answer when it is embedded in the text. Teacher guidance or class discussion will help the student find an answer.

Speed Versus Comprehension

It is not unusual for comprehension scores to decline as reading rate increases during the early weeks of timed readings. If this happens, students should attempt to level off their speed—but not lower it—and concentrate more on comprehension. Usually, if students maintain the higher speed and concentrate on comprehension, scores will gradually improve and within a week or two be back up to normal levels of 70 to 80 percent.

It is important to achieve a proper balance between speed and comprehension. An inefficient reader typically reads everything at one speed, usually slowly. Some poor readers, however, read rapidly but without satisfactory comprehension. It is important to achieve a balance between speed and comprehension. The practice that this series provides enables students to increase their reading speed while maintaining normal levels of comprehension.

Getting Started

As a rule, the passages in a book designed to improve reading speed should be relatively easy. The student should not have much difficulty with the vocabulary or the subject matter. Don't worry about

the passages being too easy;
students should see how quickly and
efficiently they can read a passage.

Begin by assigning students to a
level. A student should start with a
book that is one level below his or
her current reading level. If a
student's reading level is not
known, a suitable starting point
would be one or two levels below
the student's present grade in
school.

Introduce students to the contents
and format of the book they are
using. Examine the book to see how
it is organized. Talk about the parts
of each lesson. Discuss the purpose of
timed reading and the use of the
progress graphs at the back of the
book.

Timing the Reading

One suggestion for timing the
reading is to have all students begin
reading the selection at the same
time. After one minute, write on the
board the time that has elapsed and
begin updating it at 10-second
intervals (1:00, 1:10, 1:20, etc.).
Another option is to have individual
students time themselves with a
stopwatch.

Teaching a Lesson

Part A

1. Give students the signal to begin
   previewing the lesson. Allow
   20 seconds, then discuss special
   science terms or vocabulary that
   students found.

2. Use one of the methods described
   above to time students as they
   read the passage. (Include the
   20-second preview time as part of
   the first minute.) Tell students to
   write down the last time shown
   on the board or the stopwatch
   when they finish reading. Have
   them record the time in the
   designated space after the passage.

3. Next, have students complete the
   exercises in Part A. Work with
   them to check their answers,
   using the Answer Key that begins
   on page 114. Have them circle
   incorrect answers, mark the
   correct answers, and then record
   the number of correct answers for
   Part A on the appropriate line at
   the end of the lesson. Correct
   responses to eight or more
   questions indicate satisfactory
   comprehension and recall.

Part B

1. Have students read the Part B
   passage and complete the exercises that follow it. Directions are
   provided with each exercise.
   Correct responses require
   deliberation and discrimination.

2. Work with students to check their
   answers. Then discuss the answers
   with them and have them record
   the number of correct answers for
   Part B at the end of the lesson.

Have students study the correct
answers to the questions they
answered incorrectly. It is important
that they understand why a particular answer is correct or incorrect.

Have them reread relevant parts of a passage to clarify an answer. An effective cooperative activity is to have students work in pairs to discuss their answers, explain why they chose the answers they did, and try to resolve differences.

Monitoring Progress

Have students find their total correct answers for the lesson and record their reading time and scores on the graphs on pages 116 and 117. Then have them complete the Comprehension Skills Profile on page 118. For each incorrect response to a question in Part B, students should mark an X in the box above each question type.

The legend on the Reading Rate graph automatically converts reading times to words-per-minute rates. The Comprehension Score graph automatically converts the raw scores to percentages.

These graphs provide a visual record of a student's progress. This record gives the student and you an opportunity to evaluate the student's progress and to determine the types of exercises and skills he or she needs to concentrate on.

Diagnosis and Evaluation

The following are typical reading rates.

Slow Reader—150 Words Per Minute

Average Reader—250 Words Per Minute

Fast Reader—350 Words Per Minute

A student who consistently reads at an average or above-average rate (with satisfactory comprehension) is ready to advance to the next book in the series.

A column of Xs in the Comprehension Skills Profile indicates a specific comprehension weakness. Using the profile, you can assess trends in student performance and suggest remedial work if necessary.

The arctic tundra is an area of immense plains in the northern regions of North America, Europe, and Asia. It is bounded to the north by the polar ice cap and to the south by coniferous forests. A similar area, the alpine tundra, is found on high mountains in many parts of the world.

On the arctic tundra, summers are short and winters are long. On most winter days, there are only a few hours of sunlight. Winds are strong throughout the year, and there is little precipitation. A layer of permanently frozen subsoil called permafrost lies below the surface soil. In some places, the permafrost is 1.5 kilometers (0.9 mile) deep. Tundra soil is rocky, and because the ground is fairly level, the permafrost prevents water from draining into the subsoil. This causes ponds and bogs to develop during warmer months.

Alpine tundra is found scattered above the tree line and below the snowcaps on high-altitude mountains. The tree line marks the beginning of an area where trees are not able to grow. Permafrost is uncommon in alpine tundra, and much of the ground is very rocky. There are more hours of sunlight than there are in the Arctic.

Tundra plants, including trees, grow close to the ground. Much of the arctic tundra vegetation is evergreen, and most plants are perennials, which bloom each year. The seeds of most tundra plants can withstand unfavorable conditions for a long time. Scientists have found 10,000-year-old seeds that can still sprout and grow. To avoid freezing, some plants grow in masses. In the arctic tundra, cotton grass, sedges, small willow trees, and dwarf heather are common, as are mosses and lichens. In the alpine tundra, lichens often cover large expanses of rock.

Large grazing animals, such as caribou, reindeer, and musk ox, live in the arctic tundra, along with such smaller herbivores as snowshoe rabbits, ground squirrels, and lemmings. These animals are prey for wolves, arctic foxes, grizzly bears, and snowy owls. Polar bears also live in the arctic tundra, but only one species of amphibian or reptile—the wood frog—is found there. The arctic tundra is the summer breeding ground of many kinds of migratory birds, especially waterfowl, which feed on the many black flies, mosquitoes, and other insects there.

Animal life in the alpine tundra includes the mountain goat, big-horned sheep, pika, marmot, and ptarmigan. Butterflies, beetles, and grasshoppers are also abundant.

Reading Time _____

Recalling Facts

1. The arctic tundra is found
   - ❑ a. around the South Pole.
   - ❑ b. between the polar ice cap and coniferous forests.
   - ❑ c. on high mountains.

2. Permafrost
   - ❑ a. is a surface layer of frozen soil.
   - ❑ b. prevents water from draining deep into the ground.
   - ❑ c. is commonly found in both alpine and arctic tundra.

3. In the arctic tundra,
   - ❑ a. there are many species of frogs.
   - ❑ b. big-horned sheep are common.
   - ❑ c. there are no snakes or lizards.

4. Tundra plants sometimes grow in masses to
   - ❑ a. avoid freezing.
   - ❑ b. avoid being eaten by herbivores.
   - ❑ c. get enough sunlight.

5. The arctic tundra is a good place for birds in the summer because
   - ❑ a. the summers are short.
   - ❑ b. there are plenty of mosquitoes and other insects for birds to eat.
   - ❑ c. it is close to their winter feeding grounds.

Understanding Ideas

6. The article suggests that the alpine tundra is different from the arctic tundra
   - ❑ a. because the climate and the terrain are different.
   - ❑ b. only in the types of vegetation growing there.
   - ❑ c. because it is much colder.

7. One way in which the alpine and arctic tundra are similar is that both
   - ❑ a. get abundant precipitation.
   - ❑ b. are found in areas throughout the world.
   - ❑ c. have low-growing vegetation.

8. You can conclude that
   - ❑ a. the alpine tundra and the arctic tundra should be considered different ecological types.
   - ❑ b. animals are more common in the alpine tundra than in the arctic tundra.
   - ❑ c. both the alpine and arctic tundra are inhospitable places to live.

9. You can conclude that the most important factor for the survival of organisms in the arctic tundra is their
   - ❑ a. ability to compete successfully against other organisms.
   - ❑ b. ability to survive the harsh conditions.
   - ❑ c. similarity to organisms in the alpine tundra.

10. If a person wanted to visit the arctic tundra during the summer, he or she would be wise to take along
    - ❑ a. mosquito netting.
    - ❑ b. warm winter clothes.
    - ❑ c. sandals and a swimming suit.

14

1   B   A Wilderness Encounter

The teenagers hiked single file along the narrow North Country trail, one counselor leading the way and another bringing up the rear. They were spaced about three minutes apart so that each person could experience the feeling of being alone in the wilderness.

Roberta welcomed the cool shade of the spruce trees and balsam firs of the vast boreal forest and the soft carpet of needles on the moist trail. She kept her eyes open, hoping to see signs of life. She especially hoped to see a moose, but she really didn't want to encounter a bear, even though she knew it would probably be more afraid of her than she would be of it. At first all she saw were mushrooms—evidence of the pelting rain that had fallen earlier in the week.

Roberta passed through a moist sunken area. She felt the squishy sphagnum moss beneath her feet, its light green color a pleasant contrast to the darker green of the conifers. Suddenly she noticed a spot of bright color beside a fallen, moss-covered tree, and she stooped to look more closely. The orange creature slithered away, and Roberta continued on, smiling, the image of the tiny salamander before her eyes.

Roberta rounded a corner and came upon a sparkling stream—and something large moving among the trees.

"Hi, Roberta," her friends called to her softly, still too entranced by the magic of their time alone in the wilderness to feel like shouting.

1. **Recognizing Words in Context**
    Find the word *entranced* in the passage. One definition below is closest to the meaning of that word. One definition has the opposite or nearly opposite meaning. The remaining definition has a completely different meaning. Label the definitions C for *closest*, O for *opposite or nearly opposite*, and D for *different*.

    _____ a. allergic

    _____ b. disgusted

    _____ c. enchanted

2. **Distinguishing Fact from Opinion**
    Two of the statements below present *facts*, which can be proved correct. The other statement is an *opinion*, which expresses someone's thoughts or beliefs. Label the statements F for *fact* and O for *opinion*.

    _____ a. Walking in an area where bears live is not worth the risk.

    _____ b. Roberta saw a salamander beside a fallen tree.

    _____ c. Balsam firs can be found in the boreal forest.

3. Keeping Events in Order

Label the statements below 1, 2, and 3 to show the order in which the events happened.

_____ a. Roberta's friends greeted her with a quiet hello from beneath some trees.

_____ b. The teenagers came for a wilderness hike.

_____ c. Roberta saw a salamander.

4. Making Correct Inferences

Two of the statements below are correct *inferences,* or reasonable guesses. They are based on information in the passage. The other statement is an incorrect, or faulty, inference. Label the statements C for *correct* inference and F for *faulty* inference.

_____ a. A boreal forest is full of bright colors in the fall.

_____ b. Some parts of the boreal forest are moist.

_____ c. Few people make their homes in the boreal forest.

5. Understanding Main Ideas

One of the statements below expresses the main idea of the passage. One statement is too general, or too broad. The other explains only part of the passage; it is too narrow. Label the statements M for *main idea*, B for *too broad*, and N for *too narrow*.

_____ a. Boreal forests are found in northern areas.

_____ b. Roberta hiked through the boreal forest with a group of other teenagers.

_____ c. Mushrooms often grow after a heavy rain.

Correct Answers, Part A _____

Correct Answers, Part B _____

Total Correct Answers _____

What Is Quicksand?

Many people enjoy building sand castles at the beach. To make a good sand castle, a person must use sand that is a little wet, not dry. Dry sand is difficult to walk on, but so is sand that is saturated by ocean water. In the area of a beach between the ocean and dry sand, where the sand is wet but not saturated, a person experiences the most support beneath his or her feet. That's because the water produces a force that pulls the sand grains together and strengthens the structure of the sand. This force is called capillary force.

In each of these cases, the frictional forces between the sand particles are strong enough to maintain a relatively solid surface. But the forces are strongest when the sand is only slightly wet. In addition, the reaction forces of the wet sand pushing upward on a person's feet are about equal to the weight of the body pushing downward, so walking along the beach is relatively easy.

Sometimes sand is so saturated with water that some of the sand particles float freely within the mixture. Such a mixture is called a suspension. If there is an upward flow of water through this suspension, then the sand begins to move. The amount of pressure between the sand particles decreases, causing the frictional forces between them to decrease. The water between the sand particles prevents them from rubbing against one another. As a result, the sand does not have the strength to hold up anything resting on its surface. This is quicksand.

The major difference between regular sand and quicksand is that in quicksand the water pressure below the sand is equal to or greater than the weight of the sand particles. As a result, the water that flows upward between the particles behaves almost like a lubricant. Almost any object that lands on the surface of this sand will be too heavy and will begin to sink. However, because the density of quicksand is greater than that of water, a person lying calmly on his or her back will simply float.

Quicksand may be found in areas along rivers, streams, and lakes; in hilly areas where the ground water is not very deep and there is plenty of loose soil; and in areas with a high probability of earthquakes. In any of these areas, an underground spring bubbling up through ordinary sand creates quicksand.

Reading Time _____

Recalling Facts

1. A small amount of water pulls sand particles together because of
   - ❏ a. capillary force.
   - ❏ b. quicksand.
   - ❏ c. a suspension.

2. When there is an upward flow of water through a suspension of sand and water,
   - ❏ a. the force between the sand particles increases.
   - ❏ b. the friction between the sand particles increases.
   - ❏ c. the sand particles begin to move.

3. Frictional forces between sand particles are strongest when sand is
   - ❏ a. slightly wet.
   - ❏ b. dry.
   - ❏ c. saturated.

4. A person can float on quicksand because its density is _____ that of the human body.
   - ❏ a. less than
   - ❏ b. greater than
   - ❏ c. the same as

5. Quicksand is often found
   - ❏ a. along rivers, streams, and lakes.
   - ❏ b. only where there are no earthquakes.
   - ❏ c. in hilly areas near oceans.

Understanding Ideas

6. Quicksand is different from beach sand because
   - ❏ a. quicksand is heavier.
   - ❏ b. of the type of sand grains.
   - ❏ c. in quicksand, water flows through suspended grains of sand.

7. What might be a reason that quicksand is rare?
   - ❏ a. All state governments employ people to eliminate it.
   - ❏ b. There are not many places where water flows upward through sand.
   - ❏ c. Quicksand is not at all rare.

8. The object that would sink most quickly in quicksand is probably a
   - ❏ a. bucket.
   - ❏ b. thin, wide piece of wood.
   - ❏ c. leaf.

9. If you saw a movie scene in which people riding across a desert are suddenly swallowed up by quicksand, you could conclude that
   - ❏ a. this is a realistic scene.
   - ❏ b. this probably wouldn't happen in real life.
   - ❏ c. an earthquake would probably happen soon.

10. A scientist interested in studying quicksand would need to know a lot about
    - ❏ a. the forces between nitrogen molecules.
    - ❏ b. earthquakes.
    - ❏ c. frictional forces.

Surviving Quicksand

When walking through an area that might have quicksand, hikers can protect themselves from becoming trapped by carrying a long pole with them. Those traveling in a group should take along a heavy rope as well, and some strong fabric, such as canvas.

A person who begins to sink into quicksand should remain composed and not panic. Quicksand is extremely dense, and a person can easily float on its surface, so it is possible to survive an encounter. Once in the quicksand, the person should lay his or her pole down so that it stretches across the quicksand and touches solid ground on each side. Then he or she should lie back with arms stretched out to the sides and pull him or herself over the pole so that it is under the back, perpendicular to the spine. The last step is to gradually roll sideways toward solid ground. A person who doesn't have a pole also should try to roll sideways, because this is the only method by which one can successfully rescue oneself.

If a companion begins to descend into quicksand, a hiker can throw the victim a rope and spread out a sheet of canvas to create a surface on which to walk toward the victim. If no canvas is available, it is possible to spread out leafy branches instead, take along a sturdy pole, and slowly walk toward the stranded companion.

1. **Recognizing Words in Context**

   Find the word *composed* in the passage. One definition below is closest to the meaning of that word. One definition has the opposite or nearly opposite meaning. The remaining definition has a completely different meaning. Label the definitions C for *closest*, O for *opposite or nearly opposite*, and D for *different*.

   _____ a. terrified

   _____ b. expressive

   _____ c. calm

2. **Distinguishing Fact from Opinion**

   Two of the statements below present *facts*, which can be proved correct. The other statement is an *opinion*, which expresses someone's thoughts or beliefs. Label the statements F for *fact* and O for *opinion*.

   _____ a. Staying calm in an emergency makes it easier to think straight and do the right thing.

   _____ b. The most important item to carry with you in quicksand country is a sturdy pole.

   _____ c. An encounter with quicksand can be a great challenge.

3. Keeping Events in Order

Label the statements below 1, 2, and 3 to show the order in which the events happen.

_____ a. A hiker rolls sideways.

_____ b. A hiker gets stuck in quicksand.

_____ c. A hiker puts a pole across the quicksand.

4. Making Correct Inferences

Two of the statements below are correct *inferences*, or reasonable guesses. They are based on information in the passage. The other statement is an incorrect, or faulty, inference. Label the statements C for *correct* inference and F for *faulty* inference.

_____ a. It is a good idea to watch out for quicksand when walking along a riverbank.

_____ b. Being prepared can help a person avert disaster in an emergency.

_____ c. Falling into quicksand is one of the most dangerous things that can happen to a person.

5. Understanding Main Ideas

One of the statements below expresses the main idea of the passage. One statement is too general, or too broad. The other explains only part of the passage; it is too narrow. Label the statements M for *main idea*, B for *too broad*, and N for *too narrow*.

_____ a. A pole is needed to survive an encounter with quicksand.

_____ b. People can survive encounters with quicksand if they follow the correct procedures.

_____ c. The best way to avoid danger is to prepare for it.

Correct Answers, Part A _____

Correct Answers, Part B _____

Total Correct Answers _____

3 | A   How We Hear

Human beings constantly communicate by using sound. Each day, people encounter a series of sounds that vary greatly, from the insistent ringing of an alarm clock in the morning until the final cheery "good night" at bedtime. We receive and understand all these sounds thanks to the human ear, an amazing device that cannot be replicated by even the most modern of technologies. All sounds, from the softest whisper to the loudest music, result from vibrations that create sound waves. Sound waves travel through the air, and when they reach our ears, complicated and delicate structures translate them into a form that can be transmitted to the brain so that we can make sense of the sound.

Sound waves enter the visible portion of the ear—the external ear—and are funneled into our bodies through a passageway called the auditory canal. At the end of this passageway is the tympanic membrane, or eardrum. When sound waves strike the eardrum, they cause it to vibrate. These vibrations are transferred to the structures of the middle ear.

The middle ear contains three tiny bones: the hammer, the anvil, and the stirrup. These bones pick up the vibrations from the eardrum. Acting together, the bones of the middle ear increase the force of the vibrations and then transfer the vibrations to the oval window, a thin membrane in the inner ear.

The inner ear is made up of the vestibule and the cochlea. The vestibule helps the body keep its balance. The cochlea is a coiled bony tube that resembles a snail's shell. It is the organ of hearing. The cochlea is divided into two sections. One section consists of two connected channels that run side by side. These channels are filled with fluid, and when vibrations from the middle ear reach the oval window, this fluid begins to move in a wave motion. The inner section of the cochlea contains receptor cells known as hair cells. These cells are connected to hairlike structures called cilia. The wave motion of fluid in the cochlea causes the cilia on these receptor cells to bend. This in turn generates nerve impulses that are carried via the auditory nerve to the brain. In the hearing centers of the brain, the nerve impulses are translated and interpreted, and the person perceives a sound. In most cases, a sound is perceived less than a second after it is created.

Reading Time _____

Recalling Facts

1. All sounds originate as
   - ❏ a. vibrations.
   - ❏ b. sound waves.
   - ❏ c. cochlea.

2. The tympanic membrane is part of the
   - ❏ a. external ear.
   - ❏ b. middle ear.
   - ❏ c. inner ear.

3. All of the following are bones of the middle ear except the
   - ❏ a. hammer.
   - ❏ b. anvil.
   - ❏ c. cochlea.

4. Hair cells are found in the
   - ❏ a. external ear.
   - ❏ b. middle ear.
   - ❏ c. inner ear.

5. The oval window is
   - ❏ a. a membrane.
   - ❏ b. part of the stirrup.
   - ❏ c. connected to receptor cells.

Understanding Ideas

6. The main concept in the functioning of the human auditory system is the
   - ❏ a. transfer of sound energy in the form of vibrations.
   - ❏ b. creation of sound waves.
   - ❏ c. development of a multifaceted ear.

7. The article suggests that in order for sound waves to be heard, they must be
   - ❏ a. changed into vibrations.
   - ❏ b. transferred from the inner ear to the middle ear.
   - ❏ c. converted to a form that can be transported by the nervous system and interpreted by the brain.

8. The article suggests that if the tympanic membrane is damaged, vibrations in the air
   - ❏ a. will not be able to enter the auditory canal.
   - ❏ b. cannot be transferred to the bones of the middle ear.
   - ❏ c. will sound unbearably loud.

9. It is possible to infer from the article that modern technology
   - ❏ a. has created an artificial ear that hears even better than a natural ear.
   - ❏ b. can completely cure deafness.
   - ❏ c. has not produced an effective artificial ear.

10. It is possible to infer from the article that sound waves can travel
    - ❏ a. only through air.
    - ❏ b. only through air and liquids.
    - ❏ c. through air, solids, and liquids.

Getting a Hearing Aid

Do you know someone who has difficulty hearing in a group of friends or family members? Someone who always has to turn up the volume on the television or who avoids social events because of a hearing problem? If so, you know someone who might benefit from a hearing aid, an electronic device that amplifies sound waves and helps hearing-impaired people hear better.

The first step in getting a hearing aid is to have a medical examination and hearing evaluation. A hearing specialist called an audiologist can then determine whether a hearing aid can help and, if so, which type is best. About a thousand models of hearing aids are available. Each kind incorporates a microphone to detect sound, an amplifier to increase volume, a speaker to send the sound to the ear, and a battery to provide power.

A hearing-impaired person needs to understand that hearing aids cannot make things sound the way they would to someone with normal hearing. This is in part because hearing aids increase the volume of all sounds, even those in the background, and they do not make sounds clearer. When people first get hearing aids, everything may sound extremely loud to them because they have forgotten what normal volume is. They may need to be encouraged to continue wearing the devices until they get used to them.

1. **Recognizing Words in Context**

   Find the word *incorporates* in the passage. One definition below is closest to the meaning of that word. One definition has the opposite or nearly opposite meaning. The remaining definition has a completely different meaning. Label the definitions C for *closest*, O for *opposite or nearly opposite*, and D for *different*.

   _____ a. separates

   _____ b. brings together

   _____ c. publicizes

2. **Distinguishing Fact from Opinion**

   Two of the statements below present *facts*, which can be proved correct. The other statement is an *opinion*, which expresses someone's thoughts or beliefs. Label the statements F for *fact* and O for *opinion*.

   _____ a. Hearing aids cannot restore hearing to normal.

   _____ b. Hearing aids are the most effective way of dealing with hearing loss.

   _____ c. There are many types of hearing aids.

3. Keeping Events in Order

Label the statements below 1, 2, and 3 to show the order in which the events happen.

_____ a. An audiologist determines the most suitable type of hearing device.

_____ b. A person gets a medical examination.

_____ c. A period of adjustment is needed.

4. Making Correct Inferences

Two of the statements below are correct *inferences*, or reasonable guesses. They are based on information in the passage. The other statement is an incorrect, or faulty, inference. Label the statements C for *correct* inference and F for *faulty* inference.

_____ a. Everyone knows someone who needs a hearing aid.

_____ b. There are special hearing aids for certain types of hearing loss.

_____ c. It is unwise to buy a hearing aid without consulting an audiologist.

5. Understanding Main Ideas

One of the statements below expresses the main idea of the passage. One statement is too general, or too broad. The other explains only part of the passage; it is too narrow. Label the statements M for *main idea*, B for *too broad*, and N for *too narrow*.

_____ a. Determining if someone needs a hearing aid requires a careful process.

_____ b. Treating hearing loss is difficult.

_____ c. An audiologist can determine whether someone needs a hearing aid.

Correct Answers, Part A _____

Correct Answers, Part B _____

Total Correct Answers _____

The Classification of Living Things

Scientists believe that Earth has somewhere between 10 million and 40 million kinds of living things. They have identified only about 2 million.

In the 18th century, a Swedish botanist named Carolus Linnaeus saw the need for a system of classifying organisms. He thought that organisms should be grouped by shared characteristics, so he gave every kind of living thing a unique two-part Latin or Greek name. The first part is the genus name, and the second part is the species name. The genus name represents a group with a shared characteristic, and the species name represents one member of that group. For example, Linnaeus called the briar rose *Rosa canina*. Other roses are in the genus *Rosa*, but only the briar rose has the species name *canina*. This naming system is still used today. It allows people around the world to refer to a particular organism in the same way, regardless of what language they speak.

Scientists have expanded Linnaeus's system. There are now seven main levels of classification. In order from most detailed to most general, these levels are species, genus, order, class, phylum, and kingdom. New classification systems are based not only on structures and functions that are shared among organisms. The systems are based also on genetics.

In Linnaeus's time, scientists thought there were only two kingdoms. Eventually scientists created a five-kingdom classification system. The largest kingdom is Animalia. It has more than 1 million named species. This kingdom includes mammals, birds, fish, insects, amphibians, reptiles, worms, and sponges. The kingdom Plantae includes mosses, ferns, and woody and nonwoody flowering plants. It contains about 350,000 known species. Fungi, molds, mushrooms, yeasts, and mildews belong to the kingdom Fungi, with about 100,000 named species. As many as 250,000 known species belong to Protista. This kingdom includes protozoans and some algae. Monera includes about 10,000 known species of bacteria and blue-green algae.

Many scientists now prefer a system in which above the kingdoms there are three domains: Archaea, Bacteria, and Eukarya. This system is more precise in terms of genetics. Archaea, also called prokaryotes, are organisms that used to be grouped with bacteria. The study of genetic material, however, has shown that these two kinds of organisms are quite different. It shows, too, that bacteria evolved much later than archaea. Eukarya are eukaryotes, a more complex form of life that evolved much later and which includes plants, animals, and fungi.

Reading Time _____

Recalling Facts

1. Scientists estimate the number of species of organisms on Earth to be
   - ❑ a. greater than 40 million.
   - ❑ b. about 350,000.
   - ❑ c. between 10 million and 40 million.

2. According to the system of nomenclature developed by Linnaeus, a species name is made up of
   - ❑ a. a Latin name or a Greek name.
   - ❑ b. the genus name and the species name.
   - ❑ c. the name of the kingdom, phylum, class, order, family, genus, and species.

3. The most recently developed system of classification uses
   - ❑ a. two kingdoms.
   - ❑ b. three kingdoms.
   - ❑ c. three domains.

4. The kingdom *Monera* includes
   - ❑ a. bacteria.
   - ❑ b. protozoans.
   - ❑ c. mildews.

5. Eukaryotes
   - ❑ a. are more complex than archaea.
   - ❑ b. evolved before bacteria.
   - ❑ c. are nearly identical to prokaryotes.

Understanding Ideas

6. In the name *Acer rubrum,* the scientific name for the red maple tree, *Acer* is the name of the
   - ❑ a. species.
   - ❑ b. genus.
   - ❑ c. family.

7. Recent changes in classification systems are due to new discoveries in
   - ❑ a. medicine and physics.
   - ❑ b. anthropology and mathematics.
   - ❑ c. evolution and genetics.

8. In recent years, the ability to differentiate between organisms has increased because of advances in
   - ❑ a. evolutionary development.
   - ❑ b. technology.
   - ❑ c. the understanding of Latin and Greek languages.

9. The article suggests that Linnaeus's ideas were
   - ❑ a. unacceptable to scientists of his time.
   - ❑ b. new ideas that many scientists liked.
   - ❑ c. based on a previous system of classification.

10. It is possible to conclude from the article that Linnaeus's system of classification has
    - ❑ a. remained the same for more than 200 years.
    - ❑ b. been rejected by most scientists.
    - ❑ c. been modified by scientists as they have learned more.

Plants That Eat Insects

The word *carnivorous* usually brings to mind a gory image, such as a wolf ripping flesh off a dead caribou. But animals aren't the only carnivorous organisms. Carnivorous plants trap insects and literally digest them.

Carnivorous plants belong to the family Droseraceae, which includes four genera and more than 150 species. They are generally found in places where soil is lacking nutrients and few other plants can survive, such as acid peat bogs and sandy deserts. The carnivorous plants supplement the nutrients they absorb through their roots with a diet of insects. These insects provide the nitrogen necessary to the plants' growth and reproduction.

The Venus's-flytrap is a well-known carnivorous plant that grows in the southeastern United States. Its leaves form a trap consisting of two pads hinged together on one side and lined by long spines on the other side. If an insect lands on these leaves and touches the special receptors, the leaves snap shut, and the insect is trapped between the leaves. The plant then releases digestive chemicals that break down the insect, and its nutrients are absorbed into the plant. Once the insect is fully "digested," the trap reopens, and any dried remains blow away in the wind.

1. Recognizing Words in Context

Find the word *supplement* in the passage. One definition below is closest to the meaning of that word. One definition has the opposite or nearly opposite meaning. The remaining definition has a completely different meaning. Label the definitions C for *closest*, O for *opposite or nearly opposite*, and D for *different*.

_____ a. occupy

_____ b. decrease

_____ c. add to

2. Distinguishing Fact from Opinion

Two of the statements below present *facts*, which can be proved correct. The other statement is an *opinion*, which expresses someone's thoughts or beliefs. Label the statements F for *fact* and O for *opinion*.

_____ a. Some kinds of plants are interesting to watch.

_____ b. Carnivorous plants consume different kinds of insects.

_____ c. The Venus's-flytrap grows in the southeastern United States.

3. Keeping Events in Order

Label the statements below 1, 2, and 3 to show the order in which the events happen.

_____ a. Nutrients from the insect are absorbed into the plant.

_____ b. The trap snaps shut.

_____ c. An insect touches special receptors on the plant's leaves.

4. Making Correct Inferences

Two of the statements below are correct *inferences,* or reasonable guesses. They are based on information in the passage. The other statement is an incorrect, or faulty, inference. Label the statements C for *correct* inference and F for *faulty* inference.

_____ a. Plants cannot survive without nitrogen.

_____ b. Carnivorous plants are common.

_____ c. The Venus's-flytrap belongs to the plant family Droseraceae.

5. Understanding Main Ideas

One of the statements below expresses the main idea of the passage. One statement is too general, or too broad. The other explains only part of the passage; it is too narrow. Label the statements M for *main idea,* B for *too broad,* and N for *too narrow.*

_____ a. Plants obtain nutrients in different ways.

_____ b. The Venus's-flytrap has spines lining its leaves.

_____ c. Some plants capture and digest insects.

Correct Answers, Part A _____

Correct Answers, Part B _____

Total Correct Answers _____

How Sunlight Affects Health

During most of human history, people spent much or all of the daytime outside, farming, or hunting. Only fairly recently has this changed, and today many people in the United States spend almost 90 percent of their time indoors—a lifestyle change that apparently affects us in unforeseen ways. It turns out that we need sunlight in order to stay healthy.

The bright light from the sun affects our sleep patterns, our internal biological clocks, and our energy level. Exposure to sunlight helps our bodies process food and produce vitamin D_3, a substance that is vital to calcium and phosphorous absorption. Sunlight is necessary for the formation of melanin, the pigment that darkens the skin and protects it from excessive light. The light that enters our bodies through our eyes is involved in the production of serotonin, which regulates the constriction of blood vessels, and the production of the hormone melatonin, which affects energy levels.

The intensity, wavelength, and time of sunlight all govern how it affects us. The intensity of light outdoors on a cloudy day is about 10 times greater than the most intense indoor light, and on a sunny day it is much greater than that. Most artificial lights have wavelengths that are limited mainly to visible light. Natural sunlight includes light that has both higher and lower wavelengths than visible light does. These wavelengths are crucial to the production of melanin, melatonin, and serotonin. Plus, some research shows that exposure to morning light is needed to regulate sleep patterns.

Doctors have recently recognized Seasonal Affective Disorder (SAD) as a condition that is related to sunlight exposure. The symptoms generally include depression, irritability, temporarily weakened eyesight, overeating, lethargy, short attention span, and withdrawal from social activities. The shorter the days are during the winter, the more likely people are to suffer from SAD. Researchers have found that 10 percent of the people in New Hampshire experience its symptoms, while only 2 percent of the people in Florida do.

The signs of SAD typically appear in the fall and continue through the beginning of spring. Many people may have these symptoms to some degree, and for some people they are so severe that they interfere with the ability to lead productive lives. The best way to combat the disease is to get outdoors as much as possible during the winter months and, when indoors, to sit near windows or bright lights.

Reading Time _____

Recalling Facts

1. Many people in the United States are outdoors about
   - ❏ a. 90 percent of the daytime.
   - ❏ b. 10 percent of the daytime.
   - ❏ c. 75 percent of the daytime.

2. Exposure to sunlight darkens the skin by affecting the level of
   - ❏ a. melatonin.
   - ❏ b. melanin.
   - ❏ c. serotonin.

3. Typically the symptoms of SAD are most severe during the
   - ❏ a. winter.
   - ❏ b. summer.
   - ❏ c. spring.

4. Without enough exposure to sunlight, the human body
   - ❏ a. cannot absorb iron.
   - ❏ b. produces too much melatonin.
   - ❏ c. cannot establish a regular sleep cycle.

5. One way to combat SAD is to
   - ❏ a. go outside a lot in summer.
   - ❏ b. go outside a lot in winter.
   - ❏ c. work by a light box once a month.

Understanding Ideas

6. For someone with SAD, it is probably not a good idea to
   - ❏ a. use sunglasses often in winter.
   - ❏ b. take a winter vacation to the Caribbean.
   - ❏ c. take a walk at lunchtime every day.

7. If someone experiences lethargy and irritability in the winter, he or she
   - ❏ a. definitely has SAD.
   - ❏ b. might have SAD.
   - ❏ c. probably lives in a tropical climate.

8. According to the article, being outdoors during the winter, but only in the afternoons, is most likely to result in
   - ❏ a. a reduction in levels of melatonin.
   - ❏ b. the insufficient production of vitamin D_3.
   - ❏ c. a disruption of sleep patterns.

9. It is possible to conclude from the article that SAD
   - ❏ a. has always existed.
   - ❏ b. is a result of our modern lifestyles.
   - ❏ c. will be an even greater problem in the future.

10. SAD is probably most commonly found
    - ❏ a. in a city with many high-tech jobs.
    - ❏ b. among employees of a landscaping company.
    - ❏ c. in parts of Asian countries where most people are rice farmers.

Cave Life

Phillip had always wanted to be a spelunker—a person who explores caves. He imagined that if he ever entered a cave, he would be the only living thing inside. Boy, was he in for a surprise! He soon learned that despite the lack of light, caves are filled with a great variety of living things.

One day Phillip finally had the opportunity to enter a cave. Just inside the cave, he saw plenty of sunlight and a variety of plants that had adapted to the cool, moist environment. Going deeper into the cave, he entered an area with only a small amount of light where green plants couldn't survive but plenty of animals could. There he saw species such as raccoons, mice, and frogs that are incidental to cave life; that is, they enter caves occasionally but don't stay. He also saw trogloxenes, or "cave guests," which are species that live much of their lives in caves but periodically leave, typically for feeding. They include crickets, bats, flies, and gnats.

Phillip also discovered troglophiles, meaning "cave lovers," which sometimes live in caves but are also found in similarly cool, dark environments. These include segmented worms, snails, spiders, mites, and millipedes. Only when he ventured deep into the cave did Phillip find true "cave dwellers," or troglobites—animals that live in caves and nowhere else. This group includes flatworms and cave beetles.

1. Recognizing Words in Context

Find the word *incidental* in the passage. One definition below is closest to the meaning of that word. One definition has the opposite or nearly opposite meaning. The remaining definition has a completely different meaning. Label the definitions C for *closest*, O for *opposite or nearly opposite*, and D for *different*.

_____ a. not a regular part of

_____ b. always a part of

_____ c. a part of only at night

2. Distinguishing Fact from Opinion

Two of the statements below present *facts*, which can be proved correct. The other statement is an *opinion*, which expresses someone's thoughts or beliefs. Label the statements F for *fact* and O for *opinion*.

_____ a. Caves contain a diversity of life.

_____ b. People should be very careful whenever they explore caves.

_____ c. Some cave species are endangered.

3. Keeping Events in Order

Label the statements below 1, 2, and 3 to show the order in which the events happen.

_____ a. In the darkest recesses of the cave, Phillip sees a troglobite.

_____ b. Phillip sees a bat hanging from the ceiling of the cave.

_____ c. Phillip moves away from the sunlit part of the cave into greater darkness.

4. Making Correct Inferences

Two of the statements below are correct *inferences,* or reasonable guesses. They are based on information in the passage. The other statement is an incorrect, or faulty, inference. Label the statements C for *correct* inference and F for *faulty* inference.

_____ a. An incidental species can survive without ever entering a cave.

_____ b. Animals that live in caves can also live in abandoned mines.

_____ c. Troglobites need occasional exposure to sunlight.

5. Understanding Main Ideas

One of the statements below expresses the main idea of the passage. One statement is too general, or too broad. The other explains only part of the passage; it is too narrow. Label the statements M for *main idea,* B for *too broad,* and N for *too narrow.*

_____ a. Green plants live in the lighted part of a cave.

_____ b. Caves are unique environments.

_____ c. Caves contain a diversity of living things.

Correct Answers, Part A _____

Correct Answers, Part B _____

Total Correct Answers _____

Water is a renewable resource. Unlike coal or petroleum, which are nonrenewable resources and can get used up, water cycles constantly through Earth's ecosystems. It evaporates from oceans, rivers, and plants. It condenses in the atmosphere and falls back down as precipitation.

As the population grows, so does demand for water. As a result, even though water is a renewable resource, our planet faces a potential widespread water shortage. Some areas already have serious shortages. One main obstacle to solving this problem is that only 3 percent of the world's water is suitable for drinking or for irrigating crops. The remainder, which fills the oceans, is too salty. However, water conservation—through preservation and management of water resources—could help ease shortages.

Irrigation of farmland accounts for about two-thirds of all water usage. Most of the world's farmers flood their land at the start of the growing season or channel water through furrows. Much of this water drains away or evaporates. In the process, it may become polluted by fertilizers or pesticides. Drip irrigation systems can reduce waste to near zero and can cut water usage by up to 70 percent by dripping water directly above the plants' roots. New sprinklers that deliver water in small amounts close to the ground reduce evaporation and prevent water vapor from being blown away, cutting waste by 5 to 10 percent. Wastewater that is cleaned and reused provides 80 percent of the water needed for irrigation in some areas.

Conservation efforts are also effective in cities. When New York City faced a water shortage in the early 1990s, officials decided that conservation made more sense than building a new pumping station, which would have cost $1 billion. They gave away $295 million worth of low-flow toilets that use 6 liters (1.6 gallons) of water per flush instead of 19 liters (5 gallons). They installed water meters, checked pipes for leaks, and helped people install low-flow showerheads and faucet aerators, which reduce water flow by up to 75 percent. As a result of these efforts, daily water usage per person dropped from 738 liters (195 gallons) in 1991 to 640 liters (169 gallons) in 1999.

Water conservation is not just up to governments and farmers. There are ways that everyone can save water at home. These include turning off the water while brushing teeth or shaving, running the dishwasher only when it's full, and fixing leaky faucets.

Reading Time _____

Recalling Facts

1. Water is considered a renewable resource because it
   - ❏ a. can be used up.
   - ❏ b. is used throughout the world for irrigation.
   - ❏ c. cycles through Earth's ecosystems again and again.

2. About _____ of Earth's water supply can be used for drinking and irrigation.
   - ❏ a. two-thirds
   - ❏ b. 3 percent
   - ❏ c. 80 percent

3. According to the article, Earth
   - ❏ a. is undoubtedly headed for a world war over water.
   - ❏ b. has an unlimited supply of freshwater regardless of its use.
   - ❏ c. faces a possible water shortage.

4. The most water is wasted during irrigation when
   - ❏ a. farmers channel water through furrows.
   - ❏ b. drip irrigation systems are employed.
   - ❏ c. wastewater is cleaned and reused on fields.

5. A low-flow toilet uses
   - ❏ a. 6 liters per flush instead of 19 liters.
   - ❏ b. 738 liters per flush instead of 640 liters.
   - ❏ c. 19 liters per flush instead of 6 liters.

Understanding Ideas

6. It is possible to conclude that water conservation methods are
   - ❏ a. effective only on irrigated land.
   - ❏ b. most effective in New York City.
   - ❏ c. important for individuals as well as governments and farmers.

7. It is possible to conclude that
   - ❏ a. only industrialized nations need to enforce water conservation.
   - ❏ b. water-shortage issues are most critical in countries with economies based on agriculture.
   - ❏ c. countries with limited agriculture do not need to worry about water shortage.

8. It is possible to conclude that water
   - ❏ a. could be considered a nonrenewable resource because it evaporates into the air.
   - ❏ b. could be considered a nonrenewable resource because it can become polluted and never be used again.
   - ❏ c. could never be considered a nonrenewable resource.

9. The first step in water conservation is to
   - ❏ a. recognize that there is a need to conserve water.
   - ❏ b. show farmers how to conserve water.
   - ❏ c. install low-flow toilets.

10. If a water shortage becomes a reality, it will likely affect
    - ❏ a. only people who are poor.
    - ❏ b. only people in countries where agriculture is important.
    - ❏ c. people in most world regions.

More than 1 billion people in the world do not have access to clean drinking water. About 2.5 billion people live without adequate sanitation. The result? From 10,000 to 20,000 children die every day from water-related diseases that could be prevented.

Almost one-tenth of all food crops are irrigated by water that is pumped from natural underground wells faster than it can be replenished. The result? Some areas are running out of irrigation water.

Thousands of dams and canals have been built to move and store freshwater. Together, the reservoirs behind 3,000 of these dams hold as much water as Lake Michigan and Lake Ontario combined. The results? So much water has been redistributed that the rotation of Earth has changed slightly. Millions of people have had to relocate to allow room for reservoirs. About one-fifth of all species of freshwater fish have become threatened or endangered due to habitat destruction.

At times, so much water is diverted from rivers that they never reach lakes or oceans. For example, water from rivers that used to drain into the Aral Sea, in central Asia, is diverted to irrigate cotton fields. The result? The Aral Sea is shrinking, and many species of local fish are either extinct or close to extinction.

1. **Recognizing Words in Context**

   Find the word *replenished* in the passage. One definition below is closest to the meaning of that word. One definition has the opposite or nearly opposite meaning. The remaining definition has a completely different meaning. Label the definitions C for *closest,* O for *opposite or nearly opposite,* and D for *different.*

   _____ a. refilled

   _____ b. overflowed

   _____ c. emptied

2. **Distinguishing Fact from Opinion**

   Two of the statements below present *facts,* which can be proved correct. The other statement is an *opinion,* which expresses someone's thoughts or beliefs. Label the statements F for *fact* and O for *opinion.*

   _____ a. Lack of sanitation leads to an increase in certain diseases.

   _____ b. Building dams does more harm than good.

   _____ c. Some rivers have so much water diverted from them that they dry up before they reach the sea.

3. Keeping Events in Order

Label the statements below 1, 2, and 3 to show the order in which the events happened.

_____ a. Species of fish that lived in the Aral Sea became extinct.

_____ b. The Aral Sea began to shrink.

_____ c. Water was diverted from rivers that drain into the Aral Sea, in order to irrigate cotton fields.

4. Making Correct Inferences

Two of the statements below are correct *inferences*, or reasonable guesses. They are based on information in the passage. The other statement is an incorrect, or faulty, inference. Label the statements C for *correct* inference and F for *faulty* inference.

_____ a. Irrigation has been outlawed in areas where water is scarce.

_____ b. Proper sanitation reduces the frequency of water-related diseases.

_____ c. Building dams affects the distribution of species in local ecosystems.

5. Understanding Main Ideas

One of the statements below expresses the main idea of the passage. One statement is too general, or too broad. The other explains only part of the passage; it is too narrow. Label the statements M for *main idea*, B for *too broad*, and N for *too narrow*.

_____ a. Water is one of the most precious resources on Earth.

_____ b. Pumping too much water out of the ground diminishes underground water supplies.

_____ c. Water shortages are creating serious problems in some parts of the world.

Correct Answers, Part A _____

Correct Answers, Part B _____

Total Correct Answers _____

The Endless Struggle Between Predators and Their Prey

A predator is an animal that eats other animals, which are its prey. Animals of prey have a variety of physical features and behaviors that can help them escape their predators. These structures and behaviors are adaptations that animals have developed over time to ensure the survival of the species.

Many animals use camouflage as a passive defense against predators. An insect called a walking stick resembles a twig on a tree and is difficult for predators to see. Some grasshoppers are almost invisible when they are in front of leaves. Predators such as the tiger, whose stripes help it remain hidden while it creeps through tall grass, also use camouflage.

Some animals have defensive body structures that make it difficult for predators to eat them. Examples include the shell of a turtle and the quills of a porcupine.

Other animals use mimicry, the ability to copy the appearance or behavior of another creature, to stay alive. For example, some nonpoisonous frogs have the same bright colors as poisonous frogs. Predators stay away from both kinds of frogs. The anglerfish is a predator that uses behavioral mimicry to catch its food. It rests quietly in the water and waves a small appendage that looks like a fish. When another fish tries to eat the appendage, the anglerfish eats it.

Deer and rabbits are common examples of animals that can avoid predators by running fast. One of the fastest animals of prey is the Thompson's gazelle, which can reach speeds of about 50 kilometers (30 miles) per hour. Not all prey can outrun their predators, however. Many predators also are capable of high speeds. The cheetah, which can reach speeds of up to 100 kilometers (60 miles) per hour, can outrun any of its prey.

Many prey have survival techniques that are related to staying in groups or exhibiting special types of group behavior. Fish travel in schools and caribou travel in herds, making it less likely that a predator will kill any individual animal. In fact, a predator often will kill an old or sick animal, which may actually help the group. Some animals, such as elephants, protect their young by forming a circle around them so that the adults can fight off approaching predators. Wolves, which are predators, often travel in packs, a behavior that enables them to hunt prey that are larger than they are.

Reading Time _____

Recalling Facts

1. A predator is an animal that
   - ❏ a. eats other animals.
   - ❏ b. is eaten by other animals.
   - ❏ c. mainly eats plants.

2. Camouflage is used for survival by
   - ❏ a. elephants.
   - ❏ b. walking sticks.
   - ❏ c. anglerfish.

3. Mimicry is the ability to copy _____ of another unrelated organism.
   - ❏ a. only the appearance
   - ❏ b. only the behavior
   - ❏ c. the appearance or behavior

4. The Thompson's gazelle escapes from its predators by using
   - ❏ a. its speed.
   - ❏ b. camouflage
   - ❏ c. mimicry.

5. When prey travel in groups, it can be beneficial
   - ❏ a. only to predators.
   - ❏ b. only to prey.
   - ❏ c. to both predators and prey.

Understanding Ideas

6. Prey require behavioral and physical adaptations to
   - ❏ a. preserve their species from extinction through predation.
   - ❏ b. keep them hidden from predators.
   - ❏ c. ensure that they will be able to capture sufficient food to eat.

7. If a species developed camouflage so good that no predators ever caught any members of that species,
   - ❏ a. the adaptation would be useless.
   - ❏ b. the predator species might not survive.
   - ❏ c. the adaptation would be considered mimicry.

8. From this article, one can conclude that
   - ❏ a. only animals of prey have made adaptations for survival.
   - ❏ b. mimicry is the most common adaptation for survival.
   - ❏ c. both predators and prey exhibit a variety of survival techniques.

9. An armadillo's hard outer shell is an example of
   - ❏ a. camouflage.
   - ❏ b. mimicry.
   - ❏ c. a defensive body structure.

10. Some harmless snakes have color patterns that are similar to the red, white, and black markings of the deadly coral snake, which is an example of
    - ❏ a. camouflage.
    - ❏ b. mimicry.
    - ❏ c. a defensive body structure.

Attack—and Counterattack!

The family of zebras wandered away from the watering hole after their evening drinking time. The family—a stallion, five adult mares, seven young zebras between the ages of 1 and 3, and two foals—headed toward an area of stubby grass in preparation for sleeping. The sun was setting, a time that is generally safest for the zebras, for at dusk their black and white stripes camouflage them against the vegetation of the African scrubland.

Suddenly one of the females detected a faint but frightening sound—a lion was about to attack! She snorted stridently and screamed a warning to the others. The herd took off running at 60 kilometers (35 miles) per hour, with the stallion at the rear, but one of the newborn foals could not keep up. With the lion almost upon them, the zebras gathered together—with the newborn and the other young in the center of the group—just as the hungry lion raced forward and leapt toward its prey.

The stallion attacked, fiercely kicking the lion, but the lion did not retreat. An adult female joined the stallion in attacking the predator and caught the lion's foreleg firmly between her teeth. The lion roared and backed off, then bounded forward again. The zebras kicked and bit, hitting their attacker again and again with their sharp hooves, until at last the lion slinked off into the night.

1. Recognizing Words in Context

Find the word *stridently* in the passage. One definition below is closest to the meaning of that word. One definition has the opposite or nearly opposite meaning. The remaining definition has a completely different meaning. Label the definitions C for *closest*, O for *opposite or nearly opposite*, and D for *different*.

_____ a. quickly

_____ b. softly

_____ c. harshly

2. Distinguishing Fact from Opinion

Two of the statements below present *facts*, which can be proved correct. The other statement is an *opinion*, which expresses someone's thoughts or beliefs. Label the statements F for *fact* and O for *opinion*.

_____ a. A zebra's camouflage does not protect it completely.

_____ b. Zebras are herbivores that eat coarse grass and shrub leaves.

_____ c. We need to learn more about zebras to save them from extinction.

3. Keeping Events in Order

Label the statements below 1, 2, and 3 to show the order in which the events happen.

_____ a. The zebras bite and kick a lion.

_____ b. The zebras run from a lion.

_____ c. A foal falls behind.

4. Making Correct Inferences

Two of the statements below are correct *inferences*, or reasonable guesses. They are based on information in the passage. The other statement is an incorrect, or faulty, inference. Label the statements C for *correct* inference and F for *faulty* inference.

_____ a. Zebras travel in herds.

_____ b. Zebras depend more upon their sense of sight than their sense of hearing.

_____ c. Zebras fiercely protect their young.

5. Understanding Main Ideas

One of the statements below expresses the main idea of the passage. One statement is too general, or too broad. The other explains only part of the passage; it is too narrow. Label the statements M for *main idea*, B for *too broad*, and N for *too narrow*.

_____ a. Lions feed on several types of animals.

_____ b. Zebras have more than one defense against lions.

_____ c. A herd of zebras usually has only one stallion.

Correct Answers, Part A _____

Correct Answers, Part B _____

Total Correct Answers _____

Simple and Complex Carbohydrates

Carbohydrates are the human body's main energy source. Most of the carbohydrates that people eat come from fruits, vegetables, and grains. Dairy products are the only animal products people eat that contain a significant amount of carbohydrates.

All carbohydrates consist of building blocks of various types of sugars, called sugar units. Nutritionists divide carbohydrates into two groups, complex carbohydrates and simple carbohydrates. Simple carbohydrates contain one or two sugar units. Sucrose, the most well-known simple carbohydrate, is the type of sugar sold in boxes and bags at the grocery store. Simple carbohydrates also include fructose and lactose. Fructose is found in fruits, and lactose is found in milk.

Complex carbohydrates contain more than two building blocks of sugar. Some even contain hundreds. The sugar units are linked together to form long chains. Grains and foods that are made from grains, such as bread, cereal, and pasta, all contain complex carbohydrates. Such starchy vegetables as potatoes and such legumes as dried beans, peas, and lentils also are rich in complex carbohydrates.

Inside the digestive tract, the body breaks down all carbohydrates into glucose, a simple carbohydrate of only one sugar unit. In terms of providing the body with energy, the glucose from whole-wheat bread and the glucose from cookies provide the same energy. However, whole-wheat bread is low in fat and packed with vitamins, minerals, and fiber that are vital to the body's health. Some experts recommend that a little more than half of the calories consumed each day should come from complex carbohydrates.

Carbohydrates are especially important to athletes, because less oxygen is needed to release the energy from carbohydrates than the energy from proteins or fat. Eating lots of complex carbohydrates enables an athlete to exercise harder. This also allows him or her to recover from fatigue faster, because the body can quickly convert carbohydrates to the energy that it needs to revive. The body also can quickly convert carbohydrates to stored energy. Athletes who can exercise and train harder can perform at a higher level during competition.

Skipping a meal reduces the level of stored carbohydrates in the body and causes fatigue. Too much food high in fat also lessens the amount of energy immediately available to the body. Athletes should get almost three-fourths of their calories from carbohydrates, and endurance athletes, such as long-distance runners, should get almost all of their calories from carbohydrates.

Reading Time _____

Recalling Facts

1. All carbohydrates are
   - ❏ a. simple carbohydrates.
   - ❏ b. complex carbohydrates.
   - ❏ c. made up of sugars.

2. Fructose is a
   - ❏ a. simple carbohydrate found in fruits.
   - ❏ b. complex carbohydrate found in meat.
   - ❏ c. simple carbohydrate found in dairy products.

3. In the body, all carbohydrates are broken down into
   - ❏ a. sucrose.
   - ❏ b. glucose.
   - ❏ c. lactose.

4. An endurance athlete should have a diet that is
   - ❏ a. about one half carbohydrates.
   - ❏ b. about three-quarters carbohydrates.
   - ❏ c. almost all carbohydrates.

5. Skipping meals causes
   - ❏ a. more mental alertness.
   - ❏ b. a decrease in the amount of carbohydrates stored in the body.
   - ❏ c. better performance for athletes.

Understanding Ideas

6. To get the right amount of carbohydrates each day, it is best to eat
   - ❏ a. plenty of grains, fruits, and vegetables.
   - ❏ b. lean meat and milk shakes.
   - ❏ c. foods that are high in simple carbohydrates.

7. A meal consisting of a cheese sandwich, an orange, and a glass of apple juice
   - ❏ a. is high in carbohydrates.
   - ❏ b. probably does not contain fructose.
   - ❏ c. would not be good for an athlete.

8. The food most likely to be high in fiber, vitamins, and carbohydrates is
   - ❏ a. milk.
   - ❏ b. pizza.
   - ❏ c. corn on the cob.

9. A snack consisting of cola and a chocolate bar contains
   - ❏ a. large amounts of complex carbohydrates.
   - ❏ b. large amounts of sucrose.
   - ❏ c. very few carbohydrates.

10. From the article, it is possible to infer that for the average person the healthiest diet is one that
    - ❏ a. is almost totally carbohydrates.
    - ❏ b. consists mainly of simple carbohydrates, fat, and protein.
    - ❏ c. contains mainly complex carbohydrates and protein.

Here are some tips on how to lose weight while still following a healthy and balanced diet:

1. Eat a variety of foods, focusing on those that contain complex carbohydrates.

2. Choose a diet that includes only moderate amounts of salt and sodium, which are found in large amounts in processed and prepared foods. This also helps minimize the risk of high blood pressure.

3. Eat plenty of whole-grain products and fresh fruits and vegetables. These low-fat foods provide vitamins, minerals, complex carbohydrates, and other substances vital to a healthy diet.

4. Select foods that are low in saturated fat and cholesterol, and use fats and oils sparingly. The human body needs small amounts of fat to remain healthy. It is easy to eat too much, however, and large amounts of dietary fat and cholesterol create a risk of heart disease.

Go easy on foods high in sugars, and don't be fooled by foods containing sugar substitutes that have just as many calories as sugar. Foods high in sugar or other carbohydrates cause tooth decay, so it's a good idea to avoid snacking and to brush and floss regularly.

Be skeptical of diets that limit you to only two or three foods or that require pills or liquids. It may be easy to lose weight quickly with such diets, but it often is difficult to stay healthy and to avoid gaining the weight back.

1. **Recognizing Words in Context**

Find the word *skeptical* in the passage. One definition below is closest to the meaning of that word. One definition has the opposite or nearly opposite meaning. The remaining definition has a completely different meaning. Label the definitions C for *closest*, O for *opposite or nearly opposite*, and D for *different*.

_____ a. tending to believe

_____ b. tending to doubt

_____ c. tending to avoid

2. **Distinguishing Fact from Opinion**

Two of the statements below present *facts*, which can be proved correct. The other statement is an *opinion*, which expresses someone's thoughts or beliefs. Label the statements F for *fact* and O for *opinion*.

_____ a. A diet high in fatty foods can contribute to heart disease.

_____ b. A cheeseburger tastes better than bean soup.

_____ c. Many frozen dinners contain large quantities of sodium.

3. Keeping Events in Order

Label the statements below 1, 2, and 3 to show the order in which the events happen.

_____ a. Ivan wants to lose 10 pounds and begins a liquid diet.

_____ b. Ivan stops the diet and quickly gains the weight back.

_____ c. Ivan loses weight but often does not feel well.

4. Making Correct Inferences

Two of the statements below are correct *inferences,* or reasonable guesses. They are based on information in the passage. The other statement is an incorrect, or faulty, inference. Label the statements C for *correct* inference and F for *faulty* inference.

_____ a. People who avoid fruits and vegetables are more likely to get sick.

_____ b. Almost all foods in a supermarket are not very healthy.

_____ c. Figuring out what foods to eat for a healthy diet takes some thought.

5. Understanding Main Ideas

One of the statements below expresses the main idea of the passage. One statement is too general, or too broad. The other explains only part of the passage; it is too narrow. Label the statements M for *main idea,* B for *too broad,* and N for *too narrow.*

_____ a. Many people do not eat a healthy diet.

_____ b. Whole grain foods provide plenty of good nutrients.

_____ c. Following a few simple steps can help you maintain a healthy diet.

Correct Answers, Part A _____

Correct Answers, Part B _____

Total Correct Answers _____

Energy in the form of heat can be transferred from one object or substance to another object or substance. Heat transfer can occur by three processes: conduction, convection, and radiation. All of these processes occur in common activities.

Conduction occurs as a result of the movement of free electrons, which transport energy from a place of higher temperature to a place of lower temperature. When a person uses a metal spoon to stir hot chocolate on a stove, heat energy is conducted from the hot liquid to one end of the spoon and then up the spoon through its handle.

A fluid, circular movement known as a convection current can occur in gas or liquid as a result of conduction. Hotter, less dense liquids or gases rise. Colder, denser ones sink. When a person places a pot of water on a stove, the gas flame or electric coil heats the pan from below. The heat energy of the pan is transferred via conduction to the water near the bottom of the pan, which expands, becomes less dense, and rises to the surface. At the same time, the colder, denser water at the surface sinks down to the bottom, where it, too, has heat energy transferred to it. This movement transfers heat energy throughout the water by carrying heated water from one area to another. Convection currents also form in the air inside a house whenever someone turns on the heat or the air conditioning.

Radiation is electromagnetic energy, and it can transfer heat energy between objects, even if they are not touching. All objects both emit and absorb some radiation; however, the warmer the object, the more radiation it emits. Likewise, the colder the object, the more radiation it absorbs. If an ice cube is set on a saucer on a sunny window sill, the ice cube will absorb radiant energy from the sunlight and begin to melt. The ice cube also will give off radiation, but only a tiny amount that is unnoticeable by comparison. Objects with dull, rough surfaces are better able to both absorb and emit radiation than those with bright, polished surfaces. To conserve energy and speed cooking, manufacturers design pots and pans with dull, rough bottom surfaces to absorb radiant heat energy from the stove. Most pots and pans also have shiny sides to reduce heat emission into the air.

Reading Time _____

Recalling Facts

1. Heat transfer through the fluid, circular movement of a substance is
   - ❑ a. conduction.
   - ❑ b. convection.
   - ❑ c. radiation.

2. The heating of a metal spoon in a pan of hot chocolate occurs due to
   - ❑ a. conduction.
   - ❑ b. convection.
   - ❑ c. radiation.

3. All objects
   - ❑ a. only emit radiation.
   - ❑ b. only absorb radiation.
   - ❑ c. both emit and absorb radiation.

4. Radiation is absorbed best by objects
   - ❑ a. that have dull, uneven surfaces.
   - ❑ b. that have shiny, smooth surfaces.
   - ❑ c. that are involved in conduction.

5. An ice cube on a sunny window sill melts because
   - ❑ a. convection currents form within the ice.
   - ❑ b. it absorbs more radiation than it emits.
   - ❑ c. free electrons move from the ice into the air.

Understanding Ideas

6. When cold milk is poured into hot coffee, the milk swirls around in the coffee due primarily to
   - ❑ a. conduction of heat from the coffee to the milk.
   - ❑ b. the formation of convection currents.
   - ❑ c. heat radiation emitted from the coffee.

7. On a sunny day, wearing a black shirt makes a person feel hotter than wearing a white shirt because the black shirt
   - ❑ a. absorbs more radiation from the sun.
   - ❑ b. emits more radiation.
   - ❑ c. conducts heat from the body.

8. An old metal plate gives off more radiation than
   - ❑ a. an iron.
   - ❑ b. a new dime.
   - ❑ c. a flame.

9. From the passage, it is possible to conclude that the transfer of heat energy
   - ❑ a. is due primarily to radiation.
   - ❑ b. takes place only in your home.
   - ❑ c. is going on all the time.

10. From the passage, it is possible to infer that a microwave oven heats food by the transfer of heat energy via
    - ❑ a. conduction.
    - ❑ b. convection.
    - ❑ c. radiation.

Jeanine was sitting quietly in her bedroom, wondering what to write about for her science report. Suddenly she heard a deafening, whooshing sound. It was unlike anything she'd ever heard. She rushed to the window and saw an enormous, multicolored hot air balloon just beginning to soar over the nearby treetops. "Why is it making such a thunderous noise?" she asked herself, wondering at the same time what could lift such a large object off the ground.

Her curiosity aroused, she opened an encyclopedia to find out how a hot air balloon rises. She discovered that three factors were at work: buoyancy, the differences among various gas densities, and the effect of temperature on gas density.

As the last sounds of the balloon faded away, Jeanine began recording information for her report:

Hot air balloons are filled with helium gas, which has a lower density than air.

This gives the balloon buoyancy, which causes it to float on the air like a boat floats on water.

The whooshing sound comes from the flame that is heating the helium inside the balloon. As the gas is heated, its molecules spread apart, causing the density of the gas to decrease and the buoyancy of the balloon to increase.

Glancing out the window, Jeanine noticed that the balloon was gone, but she knew that at last her science report had been started.

1. **Recognizing Words in Context**

   Find the word *buoyancy* in the passage. One definition below is closest to the meaning of that word. One definition has the opposite or nearly opposite meaning. The remaining definition has a completely different meaning. Label the definitions C for *closest*, O for *opposite or nearly opposite*, and D for *different*.

   _____ a. ability to cool

   _____ b. ability to float

   _____ c. ability to sink

2. **Distinguishing Fact from Opinion**

   Two of the statements below present *facts*, which can be proved correct. The other statement is an *opinion*, which expresses someone's thoughts or beliefs. Label the statements F for *fact* and O for *opinion*.

   _____ a. The invention of the hot air balloon was an important historical event.

   _____ b. The cooler the air in a balloon, the lower the balloon will fly.

   _____ c. Hot-air balloons can be very colorful.

3. **Keeping Events in Order**

Label the statements below 1, 2, and 3 to show the order in which the events happen.

_____ a. A balloon is filled with helium.

_____ b. The balloon returns to earth.

_____ c. The flame is turned down.

4. **Making Correct Inferences**

Two of the statements below are correct *inferences,* or reasonable guesses. They are based on information in the passage. The other statement is an incorrect, or faulty, inference. Label the statements C for *correct* inference and F for *faulty* inference.

_____ a. Helium is not a flammable gas.

_____ b. Cooling a gas causes its density to increase.

_____ c. It is difficult to find information about hot air balloons.

5. **Understanding Main Ideas**

One of the statements below expresses the main idea of the passage. One statement is too general, or too broad. The other explains only part of the passage; it is too narrow. Label the statements M for *main idea,* B for *too broad,* and N for *too narrow.*

_____ a. Jeanine needs an idea for a science report.

_____ b. Seeing a hot air balloon motivates Jeanine to learn and write about how it works.

_____ c. Physics is a science that can help explain how hot air balloons work.

Correct Answers, Part A _____

Correct Answers, Part B _____

Total Correct Answers _____

The Life Cycle of a Frog

The life cycle of a frog varies considerably from species to species. Most frogs go through a two-stage life cycle. The female of most species lays eggs that hatch into tadpoles. The tadpoles gradually grow and then undergo metamorphosis, the process by which a tadpole's body changes into the body of an adult frog.

Frogs are amphibians. In the life cycle of an average frog, the female lays a mass of up to 10,000 eggs that fall into a body of water and are fertilized by the male. The eggs may be deposited in clumps, in films, in strings, or individually. In some species, the female cares for the eggs, but in others she leaves them alone.

Frog species that deposit their eggs in fast-moving waterways often attach them to rocks so they won't float away. Some species build foamy nests in branches overhanging ponds or placid streams, while others attach their eggs to the undersides of leaves that extend over the water so that when the eggs hatch, the tadpoles simply tumble into the water.

Frog eggs may require up to 40 days to hatch, although those found in tropical climates may hatch in as little as one day. The tadpole, which generally lives in water, has a long tail, a horny beak, and tiny teeth, as well as gills for breathing. Tadpoles are vulnerable to predators, and many do not survive.

During metamorphosis, the tadpole's internal and external body parts change drastically. The tadpole starts to grow hind legs. Soon after, its front legs appear. The tail gradually disappears, and the tadpole develops lungs and loses its gills. The mouth, digestive system, heart, and skeleton also change, and the young frog begins to consume dead insects and plants. The frog grows a long, sticky tongue that shoots out to catch insects. Adult frogs generally live for a year or two, during which time they mate and reproduce, and the entire process begins again.

Frog species vary considerably in their breeding habits and life cycles. In one South American species, the female lays only about 30 eggs. The male guards the egg and, after about two weeks, picks up those that remain and carries them around in its vocal pouch. The tadpoles live and develop in this bag of skin, feeding on their egg yolks. After they have undergone partial metamorphosis to become tiny froglets, they jump out and swim away.

Reading Time _____

Recalling Facts

1. In most species of frogs, an egg
   - ❏ a. hatches into a tadpole.
   - ❏ b. undergoes metamorphosis.
   - ❏ c. hatches into a tiny frog.

2. A tadpole breathes through its
   - ❏ a. lungs.
   - ❏ b. gills.
   - ❏ c. mouth.

3. During the metamorphosis of a frog,
   - ❏ a. only its internal body parts change.
   - ❏ b. only its external body parts change.
   - ❏ c. both its internal and its external body parts change.

4. In one South American species of frog,
   - ❏ a. the female guards the eggs.
   - ❏ b. the tadpoles develop in the female's vocal pouch.
   - ❏ c. the tadpoles develop in the male's vocal pouch.

5. What is the adult frog's main food?
   - ❏ a. plants
   - ❏ b. insects
   - ❏ c. other frogs

Understanding Ideas

6. The life cycle described in the article is an accurate description of the life cycles of
   - ❏ a. all frog species.
   - ❏ b. some frog species.
   - ❏ c. one frog species.

7. Most frogs lay large numbers of eggs because
   - ❏ a. most frog eggs and tadpoles do not survive.
   - ❏ b. frogs lay their eggs in water rather than on land.
   - ❏ c. frogs must undergo metamorphosis.

8. A possible reason that some frogs lay their eggs on vegetation hanging over water could be to
   - ❏ a. keep the eggs from drying out.
   - ❏ b. protect the eggs from predators.
   - ❏ c. ensure that the process of metamorphosis occurs.

9. The article suggests that
   - ❏ a. male frogs are more likely to care for their young than females.
   - ❏ b. female frogs never care for their young.
   - ❏ c. some species of frogs care for their young, and some do not.

10. It is possible to conclude from the article that
    - ❏ a. most frogs undergo metamorphosis.
    - ❏ b. every frog begins life as a tadpole.
    - ❏ c. most kinds of frogs live in South America.

It's a Frog! No, It's a Toad!

Jason has found himself a nice fat amphibian, and he's convinced that it's a frog—but how can he be certain it isn't a portly toad instead? To confirm his suspicions about his discovery, he should examine the evidence and then peruse this list of clues. After all, he wouldn't want to be mistaken, would he?

Does the specimen have the satiny skin of a frog or the dryish skin of a toad, with plenty of small, globular, wartlike projections?

Does the creature have long hind legs, designed for giant frog leaps, or does it have shortish hind legs, better for undersized toady hops?

Is the animal living, froglike, in water, or did it locate its home in a shady, moist place on land, which is a favorite toad habitat?

Does the critter have teeth, which would confirm that it's a frog, or is it toothless, which could indicate it's either a frog or a toad?

Did Jason see any eggs? If so, were they a mass of single eggs, usually laid by a frog, or a lengthy chain of eggs, usually laid by a toad?

No matter whether he's discovered a frog or a toad, Jason can be sure it is an amphibian belonging to the order Anura, meaning "tailless."

1. **Recognizing Words in Context**

   Find the word *portly* in the passage. One definition below is closest to the meaning of that word. One definition has the opposite or nearly opposite meaning. The remaining definition has a completely different meaning. Label the definitions C for *closest,* O for *opposite or nearly opposite,* and D for *different.*

   _____ a. fat

   _____ b. slimy

   _____ c. thin

2. **Distinguishing Fact from Opinion**

   Two of the statements below present *facts,* which can be proved correct. The other statement is an *opinion,* which expresses someone's thoughts or beliefs. Label the statements F for *fact* and O for *opinion.*

   _____ a. Toads are uglier than frogs.

   _____ b. Frogs have longer legs than toads.

   _____ c. Frogs and toads are related species.

3. **Keeping Events in Order**

   Label the statements below 1, 2, and 3 to show the order in which the events happened.

   _____ a. Observations of the amphibian were recorded.

   _____ b. An amphibian was located.

   _____ c. A tentative identification was made.

4. **Making Correct Inferences**

   Two of the statements below are correct *inferences,* or reasonable guesses. They are based on information in the passage. The other statement is an incorrect, or faulty, inference. Label the statements C for *correct* inference and F for *faulty* inference.

   _____ a. Most frogs can leap farther that most toads can.

   _____ b. Both frogs and toads are egg-laying animals.

   _____ c. Toads have tails, but frogs do not.

5. **Understanding Main Ideas**

   One of the statements below expresses the main idea of the passage. One statement is too general, or too broad. The other explains only part of the passage; it is too narrow. Label the statements M for *main idea,* B for *too broad,* and N for *too narrow.*

   _____ a. Frogs and toads are common amphibians.

   _____ b. The skin of frogs and toads differs in appearance.

   _____ c. Frogs and toads look similar but exhibit certain differences that can be used to differentiate the species.

Correct Answers, Part A _____

Correct Answers, Part B _____

Total Correct Answers _____

All organisms on Earth depend on other species for survival. In some cases, however, the relationship is direct and highly dependent. Some organisms live in symbiosis, which is a close relationship with members of other species. This bond is helpful to one or both species. Scientists have special terms for different kinds of symbiosis, depending upon whether both species benefit or one species is harmed or unaffected.

Mutualism is the type of symbiosis in which both organisms benefit. The relationship between the yucca plant of the southwestern United States and the yucca moth is a good example of mutualism. The yucca moth has a mouth part that is curved in exactly the right shape to reach inside the yucca flower and remove pollen. This moth lays its eggs inside the yucca flower. It also deliberately pollinates the plant, because pollination creates the seeds that the moth's caterpillars use for food. The moth's eggs hatch into caterpillars at about the same time that seeds appear. Neither species could survive without the other: The moth pollinates the plant's flowers, and the plant provides a source of nutrition for the moth's caterpillars.

Commensalism is a relationship between two species, both known as commensals. One of the species benefits, and one is not affected. Some commensals are so dependent on each other that they cannot separate, but others may live either together or apart. The barnacle may attach itself to the tail flukes or other part of a whale. The barnacle benefits by getting an excellent place to live: the whale is constantly on the move, and so the barnacle has a continuous stream of water that it can filter for food. The whale is probably unaffected by this relationship, although the barnacle may create a slight drag on the whale as it swims.

Parasitism is a relationship in which one organism, the host, is harmed. The other organism, the parasite, benefits. Generally, a parasite does not kill its host—at least not immediately—because the parasite would no longer have a place to live or a source of nutrients. Tapeworms are parasites that live in the intestines of humans and other vertebrates. They have suckers or hooks by which they attach themselves to the intestines of the host. This way, they can obtain all the nutrients they need to survive. In time, these worms can cause nutrient deficiencies in the host and may obstruct its intestines.

Reading Time _____

Recalling Facts

1. Symbiosis is a relationship between
   - ❑ a. two organisms of the same species.
   - ❑ b. individual organisms of two or more species.
   - ❑ c. animals and plants.

2. Mutualism is a relationship that benefits
   - ❑ a. both organisms.
   - ❑ b. one organism and harms the other.
   - ❑ c. one organism and does not harm the other.

3. Commensals can
   - ❑ a. only live together.
   - ❑ b. either live together or apart.
   - ❑ c. only live alone.

4. Tapeworms are
   - ❑ a. commensals.
   - ❑ b. parasites.
   - ❑ c. hosts.

5. The yucca moth and yucca plant exhibit
   - ❑ a. parasitism.
   - ❑ b. commensalism.
   - ❑ c. mutualism.

Understanding Ideas

6. Mosquitoes are an example of
   - ❑ a. commensals.
   - ❑ b. parasites.
   - ❑ c. mutualistic organisms.

7. Besides whales, where else would be a good place for barnacles to live?
   - ❑ a. on the bottom of a ship
   - ❑ b. in a mountain lake
   - ❑ c. at the bottom of a large puddle

8. A host is most likely to die
   - ❑ a. after a parasites has left the host.
   - ❑ b. after a parasite has reproduced.
   - ❑ c. immediately after a parasite has entered the host.

9. The article suggests that all symbiotic relationships are
   - ❑ a. harmful to one or the other species.
   - ❑ b. beneficial to both species.
   - ❑ c. beneficial to one or the other species.

10. The relationship between a loving owner and his or her pet dog could be described as
    - ❑ a. parasitic.
    - ❑ b. mutualistic.
    - ❑ c. commensal.

An Alga, a Fungus, and Two Brothers

Hassan prominently displayed his most recent painting in the bedroom he shared with his older brother. After scrutinizing it closely, Abdul asked, "It looks to me like a huge boulder, but it has so many different colors, how can it be a rock? Maybe it's a moldy doughnut."

"Don't you know that some things grow on rocks?" Hassan replied.

"How can anything survive where there's no dirt or water?" Abdul asked.

"Each color is a different species of lichen," Hassan said. "Lichens grow successfully even on dry, rocky cliffs."

"That doesn't tell me *how* they survive," said Abdul stubbornly.

"A lichen is actually two organisms that live together in a mutualistic relationship." Hassan waited for the expected blank expression to appear on Abdul's face and then added, "A lichen is an alga and a fungus living together in a way that enables both organisms to survive in a harsh environment, like on a rock or in the arctic tundra. The alga, which contains chlorophyll and undergoes photosynthesis, makes food for both the fungus and itself. The fungus absorbs water and supplies minerals. It's a convenient arrangement that benefits both organisms."

"Kind of like us," said Abdul, grinning. "I supply the jokes, and you supply the information."

1. **Recognizing Words in Context**

   Find the word *scrutinizing* in the passage. One definition below is closest to the meaning of that word. One definition has the opposite or nearly opposite meaning. The remaining definition has a completely different meaning. Label the definitions C for *closest*, O for *opposite or nearly opposite*, and D for *different*.

   _____ a. ignoring

   _____ b. studying

   _____ c. surviving

2. **Distinguishing Fact from Opinion**

   Two of the statements below present *facts*, which can be proved correct. The other statement is an *opinion*, which expresses someone's thoughts or beliefs. Label the statements F for *fact* and O for *opinion*.

   _____ a. Hassan's painting depicts a boulder covered with lichens.

   _____ b. Hassan's painting is colorful.

   _____ c. Hassan is a talented painter.

3. Keeping Events in Order

Label the statements below 1, 2, and 3 to show the order in which the events happen.

_____ a. A lichen is formed.

_____ b. The fungus grows much larger as the alga supplies it with food.

_____ c. Some fungus and alga cells begin to combine on the surface of a rock.

4. Making Correct Inferences

Two of the statements below are correct *inferences,* or reasonable guesses. They are based on information in the passage. The other statement is an incorrect, or faulty, inference. Label the statements C for *correct* inference and F for *faulty* inference.

_____ a. The fungus of a lichen cannot undergo photosynthesis.

_____ b. Lichens can often be found in moist places.

_____ c. Lichens are never found in cold climates.

5. Understanding Main Ideas

One of the statements below expresses the main idea of the passage. One statement is too general, or too broad. The other explains only part of the passage; it is too narrow. Label the statements M for *main idea,* B for *too broad,* and N for *too narrow.*

_____ a. Lichens can be different colors.

_____ b. Lichens result from a mutualistic relationship between an alga and a fungus.

_____ c. Mutualism makes it possible for individuals of two different species to survive in a harsh environment.

Correct Answers, Part A _____

Correct Answers, Part B _____

Total Correct Answers _____

An estuary is a coastal body of water partly enclosed by beaches, reefs, or islands. In an estuary, seawater mixes with freshwater from the rivers and streams that flow into an ocean. Estuaries are places of transition between saltwater and freshwater habitats. They are among the most productive areas in the world for generating new life, and they contain half of all the living matter in the ocean. They are the breeding ground and nursery for many ocean animals, such as fish and shrimp. Animals lay their eggs in or near estuaries, and their young grow in the relative safety of these habitats.

An estuary is divided into three main parts on the basis of the relative amounts of freshwater and seawater. The area closest to the ocean is primarily salt water. The middle section is brackish, or somewhat salty, water. The most inland portion is primarily freshwater. These divisions are not distinct, because the environment in an estuary constantly changes through the mixing of freshwater and seawater. As the tide comes in, the proportion of salt water increases, and as the tide goes back out, the proportion of salt water decreases. Winds, waves, and the size of the river or stream also affect the way the freshwater and seawater mix together. All living things in an estuary must adapt to this constantly changing environment.

Estuaries contain not just individual habitats but a whole mix of interconnected habitats. These connections are defined by physical factors in the environment such as the terrain, the flow of freshwater, and the tides. The different types of habitats found in estuaries include lagoons, sloughs, swamps, and salt marshes.

A lagoon is an open area of water between a small island and the mainland. A slough is a narrow estuary with very shallow water that recedes during low tides to expose areas of mud or sand. These mud flats and sand flats provide a home for clams and other animals.

A swamp is a low area—often wooded, quite large, and fairly far inland—that is often covered with water. A salt marsh is a shallow estuary protected from ocean waves and inhabited by grasses and other plants that are submerged during high tides. Salt marshes are even more productive ecosystems than rain forests and are an important habitat for a large variety of invertebrates, waterfowl, small land mammals, and insects.

Reading Time _____

Recalling Facts

1. An estuary contains
   - ❏ a. only freshwater.
   - ❏ b. only seawater.
   - ❏ c. both freshwater and seawater.

2. The environment in an estuary
   - ❏ a. is stable.
   - ❏ b. changes constantly.
   - ❏ c. changes once a day.

3. Estuaries are
   - ❏ a. extremely productive ecosystems for generating new life.
   - ❏ b. one of the least productive ecosystems.
   - ❏ c. most productive in the brackish section.

4. An estuary contains
   - ❏ a. only one habitat.
   - ❏ b. many interconnected habitats.
   - ❏ c. three distinct habitats.

5. A salt marsh habitat
   - ❏ a. is unprotected from ocean waves.
   - ❏ b. has deep water.
   - ❏ c. contains many submerged grasses.

Understanding Ideas

6. From this article, one can conclude that estuaries are
   - ❏ a. important to the fishing industry.
   - ❏ b. more important than oceans.
   - ❏ c. important only to the animals that live in them.

7. When the water flow from rivers into an estuary is heavy after strong rain, the proportion of freshwater most likely
   - ❏ a. decreases.
   - ❏ b. increases.
   - ❏ c. stays the same.

8. What might be one reason that estuaries are safer for young fish than oceans are?
   - ❏ a. It is difficult for predators to adapt to the changing environments of estuaries.
   - ❏ b. Estuaries are less polluted.
   - ❏ c. Estuaries are much warmer.

9. The proportion of salt water in an estuary is probably highest
   - ❏ a. at low tide.
   - ❏ b. at high tide.
   - ❏ c. when the wind is not blowing.

10. Because estuaries are constantly changing, it is likely that
    - ❏ a. all fish and shellfish would thrive there.
    - ❏ b. only vertebrates could survive there.
    - ❏ c. some plants and animals would not be able to survive there.

A Protected Beach

"Why can't we go onto the beach?" asked Felicity in dismay when she and her friends pulled into the parking lot, only to find a sign that said CLOSED. Reading the small print at the bottom of the sign, they quickly discovered that the beach was off-limits to humans because plovers were nesting.

"What in the world is a plover?" exclaimed Warner. "And why is it keeping me off the beach?" Although his friends just wanted to find another beach, Warner was indomitable, and he soon located a park ranger.

"Plovers are rare shorebirds that nest in the sand dunes at this time of year," she explained, "and we need to keep people out, or they'll disturb the nests, and the young won't survive. You see, sand dunes are an extremely important and special habitat, and people can easily do a lot of damage. The dunes are a critical line of defense for our shorelines during storms, and they attract and catch blowing sand and consequently build up the beaches. They are home to a wide variety of grasses, wildflowers, and shrubs, as well as sea turtles, crabs, and various shorebirds that nest here and feed on seeds and insects."

"Well," sighed Felicity, "I guess there's a lot more to going to the beach than just sitting in the sun!"

1. Recognizing Words in Context

Find the word *indomitable* in the passage. One definition below is closest to the meaning of that word. One definition has the opposite or nearly opposite meaning. The remaining definition has a completely different meaning. Label the definitions C for *closest*, O for *opposite or nearly opposite*, and D for *different*.

_____ a. accommodating

_____ b. unstoppable

_____ c. justifiable

2. Distinguishing Fact from Opinion

Two of the statements below present *facts*, which can be proved correct. The other statement is an *opinion*, which expresses someone's thoughts or beliefs. Label the statements F for *fact* and O for *opinion*.

_____ a. Sand dunes provide habitats for some endangered species.

_____ b. Sand dunes shelter shorelines from storms.

_____ c. Sand dunes should be made off-limits to people.

3. Keeping Events in Order

Label the statements below 1, 2, and 3 to show the order in which the events happened.

_____ a. The plovers began nesting on the beach.

_____ b. Warner and his friends drove into the beach parking lot.

_____ c. Park rangers decided to close the beach.

4. Making Correct Inferences

Two of the statements below are correct *inferences,* or reasonable guesses. They are based on information in the passage. The other statement is an incorrect, or faulty, inference. Label the statements C for *correct* inference and F for *faulty* inference.

_____ a. Walking on sand dunes could cause damage to the delicate ecosystem.

_____ b. Rabbits living in sand dunes feed on the beach grass.

_____ c. Raccoons are more common than birds in a sand dune ecosystem.

5. Understanding Main Ideas

One of the statements below expresses the main idea of the passage. One statement is too general, or too broad. The other explains only part of the passage; it is too narrow. Label the statements M for *main idea,* B for *too broad,* and N for *too narrow.*

_____ a. Sand dunes are important habitats for animals and plants.

_____ b. Wildflowers grow on some sand dunes.

_____ c. Many seashores have sand dunes.

Correct Answers, Part A _____

Correct Answers, Part B _____

Total Correct Answers _____

Snow Travel in the Arctic

The northern Arctic region is a land that is covered with snow for most of the year. People who live there have developed efficient ways of traveling over this perpetual snow cover. Though there are different forms of snow—ice sheets, pack ice, drifting snow, heavy falling snow—northern peoples have modes of transport that work well on all of them.

From earliest times, native peoples of the Arctic have used dogsleds as one method of transportation over snow-covered land and ice-covered bodies of water. Sled-dog breeds include Siberian huskies and Alaskan malamutes. The traditional dogsled was made out of wood, or dried salmon if wood was unavailable. The tendons of animals killed for food, such as seals and walruses, were used to make leashes for the dogs. Traditional dogsleds used a "fan" hitch, in which each dog was leashed separately to the sled. Modern sleds use "pair" hitches, in which two dogs are leashed side-by-side, and pairs are leashed together to the sled. Modern dogsleds are pulled by teams of eight dogs.

Today, in many northern regions the dogsled has been replaced by the motorized snowmobile, developed in the 1920s. Snowmobiles are small, lightweight, one- or two-seat vehicles that move on runners or skis. Snowmobiles enable people to move quickly over any kind of snow or ice. They are used for transportation, rescue, and recreation. In some northern national parks, however, snowmobiles have been banned because they are noisy and may disturb habitats.

People have also long used skis to travel over snow. Archaeologists have discovered skis that are more than 5,000 years old in bogs in Sweden and Finland. These skis are shorter and wider than those used today. Narrower wood skis are still used by people in the Lapland region of far northern Europe. Modern skis are longer and thinner than traditional ones; they are made of newer materials, such as aluminum, plastic, or fiberglass and have a laminated lower surface.

Finally, since early civilizations, people have used snowshoes, which have a wide, flat shape that enables a person to walk over deep snow without sinking. Traditional snowshoes had a light, oval, wooden frame crisscrossed with thongs and straps that held the foot. The basic shape of the snowshoe has changed little over time. But modern snowshoe frames are made from aluminum or synthetic materials, with either synthetic or leather thongs and straps.

Reading Time _____

Recalling Facts

1. The Arctic region is
   - ❑ a. in the far north.
   - ❑ b. near the South Pole.
   - ❑ c. uninhabited.

2. Native peoples constructed dogsleds out of dried salmon when
   - ❑ a. they had more fish than they could eat.
   - ❑ b. they couldn't hunt seals or walrus.
   - ❑ c. there was no available wood.

3. Traditional skis and snowshoes are made of
   - ❑ a. wood.
   - ❑ b. animal tendons.
   - ❑ c. aluminum.

4. Traditional dogsleds have been replaced in some areas by
   - ❑ a. skis.
   - ❑ b. snowshoes.
   - ❑ c. snowmobiles.

5. Which of the following are used to make skis today?
   - ❑ a. fiberglass, plastic, and wood
   - ❑ b. aluminum, plastic, and fiberglass
   - ❑ c. aluminum, fiberglass, and wood

Understanding Ideas

6. One could infer that modern dogsleds use pair hitching because it
   - ❑ a. costs less than fan hitching.
   - ❑ b. allows for better control over sled dogs.
   - ❑ c. lightens the sled's weight.

7. From the article, one can conclude that Siberian huskies and Alaskan malamutes
   - ❑ a. have adapted to cold climates.
   - ❑ b. are difficult to train.
   - ❑ c. are subjected to poor and cruel treatment by those who ride dogsleds.

8. One benefit of using modern materials to make skis and snowshoes is that these materials are
   - ❑ a. unbreakable.
   - ❑ b. flat and wide.
   - ❑ c. lightweight.

9. If someone were caught in a snowstorm, which of the following objects would be best for helping him or her move on top of deep snow?
   - ❑ a. thin, wide pieces of wood
   - ❑ b. tent poles
   - ❑ c. a large tree branch

10. You can infer from the context of the article that the word *laminated* means
    - ❑ a. covered with a layer of plastic.
    - ❑ b. provided with long, thin runners.
    - ❑ c. wide and flat to prevent sinking.

13 | B | Learning to Snowshoe

Snowshoeing has become a popular winter sport, yet this activity is at least 6,000 years old. The earliest North Americans probably arrived on snowshoes. Today the sport is increasing in popularity, so here are some pointers to help a novice get started and join the excitement.

Whether one decides to rent or buy snowshoes, it is advisable for any first-time snowshoer to select the smallest pair possible, allowing 1 square inch of surface area per snowshoe for each pound of body weight, or 5 square centimeters for every 2 kilograms. Once on the snow, the novice should simply put one foot in front and to the side of the other, using a large enough stride to make sure the snowshoes don't overlap.

When going up gentle hills, a snowshoer should put his or her weight into each step so that the snowshoes will grab the snow. For steeper ascents, the toes should be angled outward and the heels inward, or one can travel in a zigzag motion from side-to-side up the hillside. To prevent backsliding, a person should angle the snowshoes toward the slope with each step so they form level surfaces. The weight should be kept on the inside of the snowshoes to maintain a more stable grip on the snow.

Whenever a snowshoer encounters an obstacle, such as a fallen tree, she or he should step over it sideways with the weight on the forward foot first.

1. Recognizing Words in Context

Find the word *novice* in the passage. One definition below is closest to the meaning of that word. One definition has the opposite or nearly opposite meaning. The remaining definition has a completely different meaning. Label the definitions C for *closest*, O for *opposite or nearly opposite*, and D for *different*.

_____ a. beginner

_____ b. athlete

_____ c. expert

2. Distinguishing Fact from Opinion

Two of the statements below present *facts*, which can be proved correct. The other statement is an *opinion*, which expresses someone's thoughts or beliefs. Label the statements F for *fact* and O for *opinion*.

_____ a. Some strategies for going up and down hills can be useful when snowshoeing.

_____ b. Snowshoeing is a popular winter sport.

_____ c. Snowshoeing is easier than cross-country skiing.

3. Keeping Events in Order

Label the statements below 1, 2, and 3 to show the order in which the events happen.

_____ a. Once the snowshoer has found a location suitable to his or her skill level, he or she selects the smallest pair of snowshoes possible.

_____ b. The snowshoer begins by putting one foot in front of the other, using a long stride.

_____ c. A beginning snowshoer conducts some research to find a snowy area that is appropriate to his or her skill level.

4. Making Correct Inferences

Two of the statements below are correct *inferences,* or reasonable guesses. They are based on information in the passage. The other statement is an incorrect, or faulty, inference. Label the statements C for *correct* inference and F for *faulty* inference.

_____ a. Snowshoeing can be used as a means of transportation.

_____ b. Both older and younger people can enjoy snowshoeing.

_____ c. Snowshoeing is about as popular in Minnesota as it is in Texas.

5. Understanding Main Ideas

One of the statements below expresses the main idea of the passage. One statement is too general, or too broad. The other explains only part of the passage; it is too narrow. Label the statements M for *main idea,* B for *too broad,* and N for *too narrow.*

_____ a. Popular winter sports include skiing, snowboarding, and snowshoeing.

_____ b. A person can learn to snowshoe by following simple directions.

_____ c. It is important to use a snowshoe that fits well.

Correct Answers, Part A _____

Correct Answers, Part B _____

Total Correct Answers _____

14 | A | What Is the World Wide Web?

The World Wide Web is a collection of linked documents and files that are available to anyone who has access to the Internet. Born in 1992, the Web is made possible because of two other developments: hypertext technology and the Internet itself.

Hypertext uses related links, called hyperlinks, to allow a computer user to jump from one document to another. For example, if a person were reading this passage on an online encyclopedia, the words *World Wide Web* might appear underlined. If the person clicked on the underlined words with his or her mouse, an article with more detailed information on that subject would appear on the computer screen.

The Internet is a group of large computer networks that link together thousands of smaller computer networks. Governments, schools, and businesses own many of these networks, but Internet service providers also have networks, which give individual computer users access to the Internet.

Web sites are made up of Web pages, which contain printed text, graphics, audio, and even video. The opening page for any Web site is called its home page. A user can get to this page, or any other page, by typing in its corresponding Uniform Resource Locator (URL) address. Computer users can also find information in Web files by using a specialized computer program called a search engine. Users launch a search based on keywords, and the search engine searches the Internet for Web pages that contain these words. For example, if users wanted to find out when e-mail was invented, they would access a search engine and type in the words "e-mail was invented." This should bring up on the computer screen a list of links related to the subject of e-mail.

The Web functions as an enormous electronic library, giving people instant access to countless pieces of information. People can search databases and libraries around the world. With the Web, people can view pictures of an expedition on Mount Everest or famous artworks. They can also take classes. In addition, Web pages are useful on a more practical daily basis, enabling people to get up-to-the-minute news, sports, and weather reports.

Businesses also have benefited from this technology. They have created Web sites to promote their products, to sell their merchandise, and to offer various services. At the turn of this century, close to 1 billion Web pages could be accessed by any Internet user.

Reading Time _____

Recalling Facts

1. The World Wide Web is
   - ❏ a. a collection of documents and files.
   - ❏ b. the Internet.
   - ❏ c. a network of computer languages.

2. Which technology was developed before the World Wide Web?
   - ❏ a. hypertext
   - ❏ b. Web browsers
   - ❏ c. service provider networks

3. Businesses have benefited from the Web because they have been able to
   - ❏ a. advertise their products in new ways.
   - ❏ b. develop new products more quickly.
   - ❏ c. sell Uniform Resource Locator addresses.

4. Which of the following would be least likely to run its own computer network?
   - ❏ a. the federal government
   - ❏ b. a state university
   - ❏ c. an individual computer user

5. Hypertext technology relies on a system of
   - ❏ a. online databases.
   - ❏ b. related links.
   - ❏ c. computer networks.

Understanding Ideas

6. Access to the World Wide Web would be most helpful in
   - ❏ a. writing new computer programs.
   - ❏ b. writing an autobiography.
   - ❏ c. locating articles for a science report.

7. The Web offers all of these advantages *except for*
   - ❏ a. information for all five senses.
   - ❏ b. speed.
   - ❏ c. breadth of information.

8. In the future, Web pages will probably become
   - ❏ a. extremely long.
   - ❏ b. more plentiful.
   - ❏ c. highly specialized.

9. An Internet service provider is most likely to be used by
   - ❏ a. an international agency.
   - ❏ b. a typical family.
   - ❏ c. a large business.

10. The best way to find more information on the history of the Internet would be to
   - ❏ a. type in "history of the Internet" on a search engine.
   - ❏ b. look for the Internet's home page.
   - ❏ c. go to a computer company's Web site.

The Inventor of the World Wide Web

If someone did a search for "Tim Berners-Lee" on the World Wide Web, he or she could get as many as 80,000 "hits," or URL addresses. This is appropriate because Berners-Lee invented the World Wide Web.

The story of the World Wide Web begins in 1980 in Geneva, Switzerland. Berners-Lee, a British computer scientist, was trying to develop a way to organize his notes. He wrote and produced software that created a "hypertext" notebook within his computer. This program allowed Berners-Lee to link words in each document to other files on his computer.

Although the program worked extremely well, it linked only the documents in his computer. A bigger step came in 1989 when Berners-Lee propounded a global hypertext project that would allow people around the world to link their computers and, thus, their information. Berners-Lee based the new software for this project on his earlier program. He soon developed the key features of the Web, including HyperText Markup Language (HTML), HyperText Transfer Protocol (HTTP) addresses, and the first Web browser. In 1992 the World Wide Web made its debut, changing forever the way many people do business, spend their free time, exchange ideas, and keep in touch with family and friends.

And what became of Berners-Lee? Instead of cashing in on his success, Berners-Lee chose to make the Web open and free to everyone. Today he devotes his career to global Web development.

1. **Recognizing Words in Context**

   Find the word *propounded* in the passage. One definition below is closest to the meaning of that word. One definition has the opposite or nearly opposite meaning. The remaining definition has a completely different meaning. Label the definitions C for *closest*, O for *opposite or nearly opposite*, and D for *different*.

   _____ a. suggested

   _____ b. eliminated

   _____ c. weighed

2. **Distinguishing Fact from Opinion**

   Two of the statements below present *facts*, which can be proved correct. The other statement is an *opinion*, which expresses someone's thoughts or beliefs. Label the statements F for *fact* and O for *opinion*.

   _____ a. The World Wide Web should be free and open to everyone.

   _____ b. Berners-Lee developed key characteristics of the Web.

   _____ c. Berners-Lee wanted people to share their information.

3. Keeping Events in Order

Label the statements below 1, 2, and 3 to show the order in which the events happened.

_____ a. Berners-Lee wrote a program that used a "hypertext" notebook.

_____ b. Berners-Lee was able to link documents on his computer.

_____ c. Berners-Lee propounded a global hypertext project.

4. Making Correct Inferences

Two of the statements below are correct *inferences,* or reasonable guesses. They are based on information in the passage. The other statement is an incorrect, or faulty, inference. Label the statements C for *correct* inference and F for *faulty* inference.

_____ a. Berners-Lee used the same software for each of his hypertext projects.

_____ b. The Web has allowed people to communicate in new ways.

_____ c. Berners-Lee has a resourceful imagination.

5. Understanding Main Ideas

One of the statements below expresses the main idea of the passage. One statement is too general, or too broad. The other explains only part of the passage; it is too narrow. Label the statements M for *main idea,* B for *too broad,* and N for *too narrow.*

_____ a. The Internet has grown in popularity thanks to several key developments.

_____ b. Berners-Lee developed the idea and features of the Web.

_____ c. The Web made its debut in 1989.

Correct Answers, Part A _____

Correct Answers, Part B _____

Total Correct Answers _____

15　A　A Hall of Gems and Minerals

Some museums have amazing displays of bright, shiny gems and minerals in all colors of the rainbow. One such place is the Carnegie Museum of Natural History in Pittsburgh, where there are hundreds of minerals in a single room. Minerals are chemical elements or compounds that are formed by natural processes, especially those processes that occur beneath the surface of Earth. Minerals are inorganic—that is, they do not contain any material from plants or animals.

In one part of the Carnegie museum's exhibit, there are dozens of mineral samples with amazing colors and shapes. These are displayed as "natural works of art." In another, there is a display of meteorites that have landed in Pennsylvania. A display of pseudomorphs, which means "false forms," tells about minerals that have the appearance of the crystal shape of other minerals. Here visitors can see eight kinds of pseudomorphs. The museum's staff has grouped the stones according to the types of processes that formed them and the changes that they went through as they were formed.

There are more than 3,000 different minerals in the world, each with its own unique chemical makeup, crystal structure, and physical traits. In the most widely used system of mineral sorting, geologists classify minerals on the basis of the negatively charged chemical groups, called anions, that are present in the minerals.

One main exhibit features gemstones. Gemstones are minerals that are beautiful and strong. This display includes diamonds, sapphires, rubies, emeralds, and turquoise. It also has gems such as lapis lazuli, an example of a gem that is a mixture of minerals. Many of the gems have been cut and polished. They diffract, reflect, and absorb light in ways that make them far more beautiful than stones that have not been cut and polished. Some gems are not minerals, because they come from living things, so the exhibit also contains organic gems such as coral, amber, pearls, and ivory.

Many other museums in the United States also give this experience of both sheer beauty and great information. These include the American Museum of Natural History in New York City, the Field Museum of Natural History in Chicago, and the California Academy of Sciences Natural History Museum in San Francisco. Anyone who can't find a mineral collection close enough to home to visit can take a virtual tour of these exhibits on the Internet.

Reading Time _____

Recalling Facts

1. A mineral
   - ❑ a. is an organic compound.
   - ❑ b. is formed through inorganic processes.
   - ❑ c. must be beautiful, rare, and strong.

2. Every mineral has a characteristic
   - ❑ a. set of physical properties.
   - ❑ b. gemstone form.
   - ❑ c. shape.

3. An anion is
   - ❑ a. a type of atom.
   - ❑ b. a negatively charged chemical group.
   - ❑ c. an inorganic process.

4. A sapphire is
   - ❑ a. a mineral gemstone.
   - ❑ b. a combination of minerals.
   - ❑ c. an organic compound.

5. A gemstone reflects and absorbs light differently
   - ❑ a. if it is an organic compound rather than a mineral.
   - ❑ b. after it has been cut and polished.
   - ❑ c. when it is placed in a museum hall.

Understanding Ideas

6. From the article, you can infer that the word *organic* means
   - ❑ a. in a crystal form.
   - ❑ b. composed of material from plants or animals.
   - ❑ c. a combination of minerals.

7. Minerals can be gemstones,
   - ❑ a. and all minerals are gemstones.
   - ❑ b. and all gemstones are minerals.
   - ❑ c. but a gemstone is not necessarily a mineral.

8. From the article, it is possible to conclude that
   - ❑ a. there is tremendous variation among minerals and gemstones.
   - ❑ b. minerals can be classified by their organic parts.
   - ❑ c. all minerals are beautiful.

9. From the article, it is possible to infer that the crystalline structure of a mineral
   - ❑ a. can help in identifying the type of mineral.
   - ❑ b. has no effect on its appearance.
   - ❑ c. is more important than the anions it contains.

10. If a person found an interesting rock and wanted to sell it to a jewelry maker, it would be important first to
    - ❑ a. identify the kinds of jewelry desired that are popular.
    - ❑ b. find out how much the rock was worth.
    - ❑ c. have the rock cut and polished.

Mining for Diamonds

Diamonds, the hardest natural substance on Earth, are chunks of pure carbon that have been transformed into crystals by extreme heat and pressure. Diamonds form in molten rock about 160 kilometers (100 miles) under Earth's surface and then are forced toward the surface during volcanic eruptions. In most cases, diamonds are deposited in cone-shaped masses of kimberlite rock known as pipes. Massive shifts in rocks beneath Earth and the force of glaciers and water can carry diamonds far from where they are formed, into riverbeds and even into the ocean.

Originally diamonds were taken from the bottoms of riverbeds in India. Then in the 1870s, diamonds were discovered in kimberlite pipes in South Africa. To mine diamonds, workers dig a shaft in the ground near a kimberlite pipe and then build tunnels from the mineshaft to the pipe. The kimberlite is removed from the pipe and taken to the surface, where, on average, one diamond is removed from about every 20 tons of rock.

In 1955 scientists learned how to make synthetic diamonds in a laboratory by subjecting graphite, a soft form of carbon, to extreme pressure and heat. Since the 1960s, diamonds have been mined off the coast of Namibia, Africa. A long rubber hose is lowered from a barge to the sea floor, and the hose sucks up gravel that contains approximately one diamond per ton of gravel.

1. **Recognizing Words in Context**

Find the word *synthetic* in the passage. One definition below is closest to the meaning of that word. One definition has the opposite or nearly opposite meaning. The remaining definition has a completely different meaning. Label the definitions C for *closest*, O for *opposite or nearly opposite*, and D for *different*.

_____ a. manufactured

_____ b. insincere

_____ c. natural

2. **Distinguishing Fact from Opinion**

Two of the statements below present *facts*, which can be proved correct. The other statement is an *opinion*, which expresses someone's thoughts or beliefs. Label the statements F for *fact* and O for *opinion*.

_____ a. Diamonds are the hardest natural substance on Earth.

_____ b. Many workers are needed to make diamond mining possible.

_____ c. Diamonds are the most beautiful stone on Earth.

3. Keeping Events in Order

Label the statements below 1, 2, and 3 to show the order in which the events happen.

_____ a. Scientists learn how to make synthetic diamonds in the laboratory.

_____ b. Diamonds are discovered in South Africa.

_____ c. Diamonds form about 160 kilometers below Earth's surface.

4. Making Correct Inferences

Two of the statements below are correct *inferences*, or reasonable guesses. They are based on information in the passage. The other statement is an incorrect, or faulty, inference. Label the statements C for *correct* inference and F for *faulty* inference.

_____ a. Diamonds are not found in many places on Earth.

_____ b. Diamond mining is a complex process.

_____ c. The world's supply of diamonds will soon run out.

5. Understanding Main Ideas

One of the statements below expresses the main idea of the passage. One statement is too general, or too broad. The other explains only part of the passage; it is too narrow. Label the statements M for *main idea*, B for *too broad*, and N for *too narrow*.

_____ a. Diamonds are one of many valuable gems mined from the earth.

_____ b. Diamonds come from several different sources.

_____ c. South Africa is an important source of diamonds.

Correct Answers, Part A _____

Correct Answers, Part B _____

Total Correct Answers _____

Microbes and Germs

Microbes and germs are tiny organisms that include bacteria, viruses, fungi, and protozoa. These kinds of organisms are called microorganisms, and they are so small that microscopes are needed to see them.

Bacteria are one-celled organisms that are round, rod-shaped, spiral, or curved. Many people think of bacteria as things that cause disease. Of the more than 1,600 known species of bacteria, however, fewer than 200 species make people sick. Some bacteria, such as intestinal bacteria, are actually helpful. Intestinal bacteria aid in digestion, and other kinds of bacteria help prevent infections.

Harmful bacteria are commonly spread from four sources: impure water and food, the tiny drops of fluid in a sick person's cough or sneeze, dirty hands, or contaminated surfaces. Human diseases caused by bacteria include tuberculosis, tetanus, and leprosy, but antibiotics have been helpful in controlling the spread and severity of some bacterial diseases.

Viruses are submicroscopic; they are much smaller than bacteria. Viruses come in many different shapes: some are 20-sided polygons, some are rod-shaped, and some even appear to have a head and a tail. By themselves, viruses are lifeless, but once they are absorbed by a living body, called a host, they can grow and reproduce. They use their host's cells to duplicate themselves and infect other cells nearby.

Viruses are a major cause of disease, and many viruses are spread through droplets produced by coughing and sneezing. Viruses cause such illnesses as chicken pox, influenza, and AIDS. The only known way to prevent viral disease is through the use of vaccines, but vaccines have not been developed to protect humans from most viruses.

Fungi draw their nutrition from nearby plants and animals. When they feed on living plants and animals instead of dead ones, fungi are called parasites. Yeast, a single-celled organism, is an example of a fungus. Fungi like warm, damp places, so they often grow on moist parts of the human body, such as between the toes or in the breathing passages. Athlete's foot is one human illness caused by a fungus, but antifungal creams applied to the skin can clear up athlete's foot.

Protozoa are one-celled organisms. Only a few of the 30,000 species of protozoa cause disease in humans. Protozoa that cause disease are usually spread through contaminated water and food or dirty hands. Protozoa cause malaria, which can be treated with prescription drugs, but the disease still kills many people every year.

Reading Time _____

Recalling Facts

1. Some bacteria contribute to the body's function by
   - ❏ a. causing cells to reproduce.
   - ❏ b. helping to prevent infection.
   - ❏ c. killing viruses.

2. Viruses and bacteria both are often spread through
   - ❏ a. the fluid in coughs and sneezes.
   - ❏ b. boiled water.
   - ❏ c. weeds.

3. The smallest types of microorganisms are
   - ❏ a. bacteria.
   - ❏ b. fungi.
   - ❏ c. viruses.

4. In order for a virus to reproduce, it must
   - ❏ a. feed on a living animal.
   - ❏ b. be absorbed by a host body.
   - ❏ c. find a warm, damp place.

5. How are bacteria and protozoa alike?
   - ❏ a. Both are one-celled organisms.
   - ❏ b. Both cause millions of human diseases.
   - ❏ c. Both are always parasitic.

Understanding Ideas

6. You can infer from the article that the kind of microbe most dangerous to humans is a
   - ❏ a. virus.
   - ❏ b. protozoan.
   - ❏ c. fungus.

7. Which statement represents an accurate conclusion about microbes and germs?
   - ❏ a. They cause similar diseases.
   - ❏ b. They come in only a few shapes.
   - ❏ c. They vary in size.

8. You can conclude that many people die from malaria even though there are drugs that cure it because
   - ❏ a. in some countries it is hard to obtain the drugs.
   - ❏ b. most people take incorrect doses of the drugs.
   - ❏ c. doctors often are not able to recognize the symptoms of malaria.

9. From the article, it is possible to conclude that if scientists had not developed antibiotics,
   - ❏ a. there would be more cases of chicken pox.
   - ❏ b. bacterial diseases would kill more people.
   - ❏ c. all fungi would be parasitic.

10. Which of the following statements is true about viruses?
    - ❏ a. They use the host organism's cells to reproduce themselves.
    - ❏ b. They can be treated with prescription drugs.
    - ❏ c. Viruses can be prevented by eating well and exercising regularly.

Growing Bread Mold

Most people are familiar with mold as that black, green, or white stuff found on stale bread, but many do not know that mold, a type of fungus, is a living organism that grows and reproduces. The following experiment corroborates the theory that mold reproduces on food that is not refrigerated more quickly than on food that is refrigerated.

The following items are needed to conduct this experiment: two pieces of white bread (fresh bread works best), a small glass of tap water, an eyedropper, and two resealable sandwich bags. Because mold does not grow overnight, this experiment works best over a period of at least one week.

After placing the slices of bread side by side on a flat surface, use the eyedropper to sprinkle about 20 drops of tap water on each slice. Next, put one slice of bread in a sandwich bag. After ensuring that the bag is properly sealed, place it in a dark, warm place, such as a kitchen cupboard. Put the other slice of bread in a sandwich bag as well, sealing the bag tightly. Place this second bag in the refrigerator.

After seven days have passed, retrieve both bags, keeping them sealed. Examine the slices of bread. If the experiment is done correctly, plenty of mold should appear on the slice of bread from the cupboard, but far less mold should cover the slice of bread from the refrigerator. After the experiment has been completed, the bags should be thrown away without being opened.

1. Recognizing Words in Context

Find the word *corroborates* in the passage. One definition below is closest to the meaning of that word. One definition has the opposite or nearly opposite meaning. The remaining definition has a completely different meaning. Label the definitions C for *closest*, O for *opposite or nearly opposite*, and D for *different*.

_____ a. confirms

_____ b. contradicts

_____ c. forms

2. Distinguishing Fact from Opinion

Two of the statements below present *facts*, which can be proved correct. The other statement is an *opinion*, which expresses someone's thoughts or beliefs. Label the statements F for *fact* and O for *opinion*.

_____ a. Mold is a living organism.

_____ b. The bread slices need to be moist when they are put in the bags.

_____ c. Impatient people won't like this experiment.

3. Keeping Events in Order

Label the statements below 1, 2, and 3 to show the order in which the steps should be completed.

_____ a. Sprinkle water on each slice of bread.

_____ b. Place the bread on a flat surface.

_____ c. Seal the bags.

4. Making Correct Inferences

Two of the statements below are correct *inferences*, or reasonable guesses. They are based on information in the passage. The other statement is an incorrect, or faulty, inference. Label the statements C for *correct* inference and F for *faulty* inference.

_____ a. Mold will not grow in a cool location.

_____ b. Patience is a good quality for a scientist to have.

_____ c. A trip to the grocery store might be necessary before starting the experiment.

5. Understanding Main Ideas

One of the statements below expresses the main idea of the passage. One statement is too general, or too broad. The other explains only part of the passage; it is too narrow. Label the statements M for *main idea*, B for *too broad*, and N for *too narrow*.

_____ a. Mold will have grown on the bread a week after the experiment is begun.

_____ b. This experiment shows that mold grows more quickly in warmer temperatures.

_____ c. Mold is a type of fungus.

Correct Answers, Part A _____

Correct Answers, Part B _____

Total Correct Answers _____

The Many Faces of Primatologists

Primatologists come from many professional backgrounds. They may be trained as teachers, doctors, veterinarians, or something else entirely. They may study animal life, human culture, or human behavior, but what they share is an interest in primates. They study nonhuman primates, such as apes and monkeys. Because primates are our closest genetic relatives, research on primates often sheds light on human behavior and biology.

The science of primatology began in the 1920s. Fieldwork in primatology involves studying primates in their native habitats. In 1931 Clarence Ray Carpenter launched his research on howler monkeys on an island in Central America. A surge of fieldwork took place in the late 1950s. Jane Goodall, who went to Africa in 1960 to study chimpanzees, changed primatology forever. She obtained information by immersing herself in the animals' world. She ate their food, saw them as individuals, and befriended them. Although her methods were ridiculed at first, they are now used around the world.

Primatologists who observe primates in their natural habitat look for signs of power structures, social relationships, communication methods, and ability to use tools. As the scientists learn about animal habits, they come to know more about human conduct. Barbara Smuts, for example, has studied female baboons for many years. She hopes to use her work to better understand violence against women in human culture—and perhaps reduce it.

Other people work with primates in zoos and laboratories. Some focus on structures of the body, such as cells and organs. They hope to apply the knowledge that they gain to their research on the human body. Studies on the brain of the rhesus monkey have taught scientists how the human brain works and how humans see. From apes, they have learned about diseases such as AIDS and natural processes such as reproduction. Primate research has also produced many pharmaceutical treatments, including the yellow fever vaccine in 1951 and the polio vaccine in 1954. Some primate research is considered controversial because primates have become ill or died in laboratories.

Some primatologists have used their work to promote efforts to save animal species. Others focus on the primates' place in their ecosystems. Still others want to further their knowledge of human evolution. One question they ask is why humans started walking on two legs. Some primates do walk on two legs from time to time, and studying this behavior may help in understanding how humans developed it.

Reading Time _____

Recalling Facts

1. Understanding primate behavior and biology sheds light on human behavior and biology mainly because primates
   - ❑ a. get along well with humans.
   - ❑ b. walk on two legs from time to time.
   - ❑ c. share genetic similarities with humans.

2. Clarence Ray Carpenter began studying howler monkeys in
   - ❑ a. the 1920s.
   - ❑ b. the 1930s.
   - ❑ c. the 1960s.

3. Research on which of the following animals most contributed to science's understanding of the human brain?
   - ❑ a. the baboon
   - ❑ b. the chimpanzee
   - ❑ c. the rhesus monkey

4. Barbara Smuts's ultimate goal in studying baboons is to learn more about
   - ❑ a. violence against women.
   - ❑ b. the evolution of humans.
   - ❑ c. the role of baboons in the ecosystem.

5. Primatologists who work primarily in the field, or in natural settings, probably focus their attention on all of the following *except*
   - ❑ a. social relationships.
   - ❑ b. cell structure.
   - ❑ c. communication methods.

Understanding Ideas

6. The article implies that between 1920 and 1959, primatologists doing fieldwork
   - ❑ a. studied primates in laboratories.
   - ❑ b. lived in primate communities.
   - ❑ c. lived outside of primate communities.

7. Why might Jane Goodall's methods have been ridiculed at first?
   - ❑ a. People didn't like Goodall.
   - ❑ b. Her methods were new.
   - ❑ c. Her methods didn't work.

8. With which statement would primatologists be most likely to agree?
   - ❑ a. The best preparation for fieldwork is to study human biology.
   - ❑ b. Animal conservation is a less important goal than developing a better understanding of humans.
   - ❑ c. Current research may influence future generations of humans and other animals.

9. You can conclude from the article that one of the most important figures in the evolution of primatology is
   - ❑ a. Jane Goodall.
   - ❑ b. Barbara Smuts.
   - ❑ c. Cynthia Moss.

10. In the 1950s, field researchers probably
    - ❑ a. focused on the group and social relationships of primates.
    - ❑ b. preferred to investigate primates in lab settings.
    - ❑ c. were not interested in communicating with primates.

Among the Gorillas

Dian Fossey, the first human to be accepted into a community of gorillas, spent nearly 20 years in the shadow of the Virunga Volcanoes in Rwanda in eastern Africa studying these awesome animals. Initially Fossey heeded the advice of earlier primatologists. She hid herself and watched the gorillas only from a distance. After renouncing this tactic, she began to approach the gorillas on her hands and knees. She imitated their behaviors and their sounds, communicating her curiosity. Her efforts were well worth the trouble. In early 1970, after she had been in Africa for three years, a gorilla she called Peanuts reached out and touched her hand.

On her rare trips away from the mountains, Fossey was uncomfortable around humans. Sometimes she walked like a gorilla, bent over with hands hanging down by her knees. On a TV talk show, Fossey announced that she spoke to the gorillas in their language and then asked some of the other guests, "Naoom?"

However, the world that Fossey and her gorillas shared was threatened by poachers. Poachers sold gorilla babies to Western zoos and killed gorillas to obtain their heads and hands as trophies. Although Fossey called her anti-poaching efforts "active conservation," poachers called it war. In 1985 Fossey was murdered, probably by an angry poacher. She was buried at the camp she had built, and on her grave marker were the words "No one loved gorillas more."

1. Recognizing Words in Context

Find the word *renouncing* in the passage. One definition below is closest to the meaning of that word. One definition has the opposite or nearly opposite meaning. The remaining definition has a completely different meaning. Label the definitions C for *closest*, O for *opposite or nearly opposite*, and D for *different*.

_____ a. supporting

_____ b. abandoning

_____ c. researching

2. Distinguishing Fact from Opinion

Two of the statements below present *facts*, which can be proved correct. The other statement is an *opinion*, which expresses someone's thoughts or beliefs. Label the statements F for *fact* and O for *opinion*.

_____ a. Fossey's efforts were well worth her trouble.

_____ b. Fossey began to take on some of the behaviors of gorillas.

_____ c. Fossey sometimes spoke in the gorilla's language to other humans.

3. Keeping Events in Order

Label the statements below 1, 2, and 3 to show the order in which the events happen.

_____ a. A gorilla named Peanuts reaches out and touches Fossey's hand.

_____ b. Fossey hides herself to observe the gorillas.

_____ c. Fossey crawls toward the gorillas.

4. Making Correct Inferences

Two of the statements below are correct *inferences,* or reasonable guesses. They are based on information in the passage. The other statement is an incorrect, or faulty, inference. Label the statements C for *correct* inference and F for *faulty* inference.

_____ a. Peanuts was Fossey's favorite gorilla.

_____ b. Fossey wanted to make the gorillas think she was one of them.

_____ c. Fossey preferred the company of gorillas to humans.

5. Understanding Main Ideas

One of the statements below expresses the main idea of the passage. One statement is too general, or too broad. The other explains only part of the passage; it is too narrow. Label the statements M for *main idea,* B for *too broad,* and N for *too narrow.*

_____ a. Fossey's efforts to protect the gorillas probably led to her death.

_____ b. Fossey developed a strong relationship with the gorillas in the mountains of Rwanda.

_____ c. Since the 1920's, the study of primates has led to important discoveries.

Correct Answers, Part A _____

Correct Answers, Part B _____

Total Correct Answers _____

The Physics of the Plastic Flying Disc

Many people enjoy tossing a flying disc back and forth on a sunny day. Plastic flying discs are essentially spinning wings. They are able to remain in the air for several seconds because of lift and rotational stability.

Two forces work together to cause the disc to rise into the air and give it the necessary aerodynamic lift. As the disc moves forward, it divides the air rushing toward it: the airstream that passes upward, along the rounded edge of the disc, speeds up, while the airstream that travels underneath the disc moves far more slowly. The resulting difference in air pressure causes the disc to rise; the disc basically is sucked up into the air. Additionally, as the disc shoots through the air, its leading edge is tipped upward, which pushes the lower airstream down beneath the disc. However, even as the flying disc is deflecting the air downward, this same air pushes upward.

Lift, however, is not the only requirement for successful flight; the rotating motion of the disc is equally important. The spinning motion generated by the throw is what keeps the flying disc stable. This rotation gives it angular momentum; the greater the angular momentum, the more likely the flying disc will be to stay on track and continue spinning. If you throw a plastic disc, you can see angular momentum in action. A flying disc with spin is more likely to travel farther in the direction in which it was thrown, but a flying disc without spin will wobble and even tumble out of the air like a leaf. Additionally, the rotating motion of the spin gives it orientational stability; this means the flying disc will receive a steady lift from the air and thus keep moving in a constant direction. Because of these multiple factors, the faster a flying disc spins, the more stable its flight becomes.

Toy manufacturers often construct flying discs in ways that take advantage of these laws of physics. They make the discs with thick, curved edges, which maximize angular momentum and allow for maximum spin. The design of some flying discs places the lift almost perfectly at the disc's center. Flying discs can also have tiny ridges on their top surfaces, which create small amounts of turbulence. This turbulence helps to keep the upper airstream attached to the flying disc, allowing it to travel farther.

Reading Time _____

Recalling Facts

1. Some flying discs are constructed so that
   - ❑ a. they are thicker at the edges.
   - ❑ b. they fly perfectly level.
   - ❑ c. the lift is at their leading edge.

2. A flying disc's rotation gives it
   - ❑ a. angular momentum.
   - ❑ b. aerodynamic lift.
   - ❑ c. maximum spin.

3. Air that passes along the curved surface of a flying disc
   - ❑ a. slows down.
   - ❑ b. speeds up.
   - ❑ c. rises straight up.

4. The air pressure below and above a moving flying disc
   - ❑ a. remains constant.
   - ❑ b. is usually the same.
   - ❑ c. is always different.

5. A flying disc that is stable will
   - ❑ a. travel slowly.
   - ❑ b. move in a constant direction.
   - ❑ c. stay attached to the upper airstream.

Understanding Ideas

6. If a flying disc did not have curved edges, it would
   - ❑ a. fly faster.
   - ❑ b. not have as much lift.
   - ❑ c. fall straight down.

7. A flying disc that is traveling through the air can best be compared to
   - ❑ a. an airplane wheel.
   - ❑ b. a falling leaf.
   - ❑ c. a bird's wing.

8. Flying discs are designed
   - ❑ a. to take advantage of the laws of physics.
   - ❑ b. by accident.
   - ❑ c. to work electronically.

9. From the article, you can infer that if a flying disc is wobbling in the air, the disc does not have enough
   - ❑ a. spin.
   - ❑ b. lift.
   - ❑ c. ridges on its surface.

10. It is possible to conclude from the article that one necessity for flight is
    - ❑ a. turbulence.
    - ❑ b. orientation.
    - ❑ c. stability.

Training a Dog to Catch a Flying Disc

By following a few simple steps, you can train almost any dog to catch a flying disc. First, the dog must become accustomed to retrieval and must associate the disc with positive experiences. So to begin instruction, do not throw the flying disc immediately; instead, roll it along the ground like a wheel and encourage the dog to go after it.

After the dog successfully retrieves a few "rollers," give it some praise and continue the training by getting it to take the disc out of your hand. Hold the flying disc above the dog's head so that the dog will jump up and take the disc. Then, while encouraging it to grab the disc again, lead it forward with the disc.

Next, focus on getting the dog to catch the disc. Standing close to the dog, flip the disc a short distance into the air and call out to the dog to catch the disc, which it will probably do intuitively. Again, leading the dog with the disc, flip the disc into the air before it grabs the disc from your hand. Gradually increase the distance of your tosses, making sure to throw the disc high enough so that the dog can catch it before it touches ground and also being careful not to throw the disc directly at the dog.

1. **Recognizing Words in Context**

   Find the word *intuitively* in the passage. One definition below is closest to the meaning of that word. One definition has the opposite or nearly opposite meaning. The remaining definition has a completely different meaning. Label the definitions C for *closest,* O for *opposite or nearly opposite,* and D for *different.*

   _____ a. by learning

   _____ b. by instinct

   _____ c. by accident

2. **Distinguishing Fact from Opinion**

   Two of the statements below present *facts,* which can be proved correct. The other statement is an *opinion,* which expresses someone's thoughts or beliefs. Label the statements F for *fact* and O for *opinion.*

   _____ a. The distance that the disc is tossed should be increased gradually.

   _____ b. It is simple to train a dog to catch a flying disc.

   _____ c. The first step is to roll the flying disc along the ground.

3. Keeping Events in Order

Label the statements below 1, 2, and 3 to show the order in which the steps should be completed.

_____ a. Stand close to the dog.

_____ b. Encourage the dog to get the disc that is rolling on the ground.

_____ c. Flip the disc a short distance into the air.

4. Making Correct Inferences

Two of the statements below are correct *inferences,* or reasonable guesses. They are based on information in the passage. The other statement is an incorrect, or faulty, inference. Label the statements C for *correct* inference and F for *faulty* inference.

_____ a. Many dogs like to play with flying discs.

_____ b. If a dog does not behave while being trained, it still should be praised.

_____ c. The training sessions should not be overly long.

5. Understanding Main Ideas

One of the statements below expresses the main idea of the passage. One statement is too general, or too broad. The other explains only part of the passage; it is too narrow. Label the statements M for *main idea,* B for *too broad,* and N for *too narrow.*

_____ a. A dog needs to have positive experiences when being trained to catch a flying disc.

_____ b. To train a dog to catch a flying disc, follow a few simple steps.

_____ c. Dogs can be trained to do many things.

Correct Answers, Part A _____

Correct Answers, Part B _____

Total Correct Answers _____

World Population Growth and Its Effects

The world's human population did not reach 1 billion people until 1830, about two million years after human beings first appeared on Earth. By 1930 the population had doubled, by 1960 it had reached 3 billion, and by 1975 it had passed 4 billion. It took just eleven more years to reach 5 billion, and in 1999, it topped 6 billion. This fast growth is largely due to advances in medicine, mass vaccinations, and better sanitation.

Human population growth has affected the planet in many ways. One of these is the depletion of the world's forests. In developing countries, many people cut down trees every day in order to have wood to cook their food and heat their homes. Around the world, paper usage has increased drastically in recent decades, and about 3 tons of trees are needed to make 1 ton of paper.

Cutting down forests leads to erosion of soil, and once the topsoil is gone, land is no longer fertile. Soil also loses precious nutrients due to misuse and chemical pollution. The loss of fertile soil makes it harder for people to produce the food crops needed for survival.

In addition, industrialized societies need large amounts of energy, including fossil fuels. Burning fossil fuels for energy pollutes the air with carbon dioxide and other gases, which in turn affects the climate.

The increasing population also affects oceans, lakes, and rivers. Coastal wetlands—vital as nurseries for fish—have diminished. In some areas, so many fish are being caught that some species are threatened with extinction. Factory wastes and farm pesticides are polluting rivers and lakes. This pollution has destroyed habitats for plants and animals.

The rapidly expanding population has resulted in increased demand for food and water. Sixty-four countries cannot produce enough food to keep up with their growing populations. The world population is expected to reach 8 billion by the year 2025, and 3 billion of these people may face chronic water shortages.

Yet despite this gloomy outlook, people are finding ways to help those most at risk to adapt, increasing their chances for survival. For example, wastewater is being treated and used to irrigate crops. Alternate sources of energy, such as wind and solar power, are being used more and more. Old farming techniques that preserve both water and soil are being adapted for modern farms. Coastal habitats are being replanted and protected.

Reading Time _____

Recalling Facts

1. In 1999 the world's population reached
   - ❏ a. 1 billion.
   - ❏ b. 4 billion.
   - ❏ c. 6 billion.

2. One factor that has contributed to the rise in population has been
   - ❏ a. global warming.
   - ❏ b. mass vaccinations.
   - ❏ c. consumption of fossil fuels.

3. One reason for the destruction of forests is the
   - ❏ a. high demand for paper.
   - ❏ b. use of solar power.
   - ❏ c. increase in irrigation.

4. By 2025 the world population is expected to reach
   - ❏ a. 6 billion.
   - ❏ b. 8 billion.
   - ❏ c. 3 billion.

5. One way that people are trying to offset the results of a quickly expanding population growth is by using
   - ❏ a. fossil fuels for energy.
   - ❏ b. spring water for irrigation.
   - ❏ c. old farming techniques.

Understanding Ideas

6. The destruction of coastal ecosystems
   - ❏ a. causes a decline in fish populations.
   - ❏ b. is mainly a problem for the resort industry.
   - ❏ c. affects only people who live on the coasts.

7. It can be inferred from the article that problems related to world population growth
   - ❏ a. should be solved by the year 2025.
   - ❏ b. can be solved by producing larger crops.
   - ❏ c. are challenging but potentially solvable.

8. In some parts of the world, if people stop cutting down trees
   - ❏ a. people will probably die from starvation or cold.
   - ❏ b. more species will become extinct.
   - ❏ c. ancient farming techniques will become more useful.

9. The world's population reached 5 billion in
   - ❏ a. 1975.
   - ❏ b. 1999.
   - ❏ c. 1986.

10. It can be inferred from the article that population growth
    - ❏ a. is a problem mainly because of how it affects the planet.
    - ❏ b. will probably be less of a problem in the future.
    - ❏ c. can easily be prevented.

The world's largest population centers are no longer considered to be cities by some population experts. These experts are using the term megacities for places with more than 10 million people. Tokyo, with 26 million people, is the world's largest megacity. Los Angeles; New York City; and Bombay, India, also are megacities, as are Mexico City; Buenos Aires, Argentina; and Shanghai, China.

The populations of megacities in the developing world are surpassing those in developed countries, such as the United States. The size of many large Asian cities is rising especially fast. Bombay will soon be the largest metropolis in the world. Karachi, Pakistan; Dhaka, Bangladesh; Jakarta, Indonesia; and Delhi, India are expected to replace other cities on the list of the 10 most populated cities. These Asian cities share one thing in common—they are in some of the world's poorest countries.

At least one-fourth of the people living in most megacities are very poor. Unable to pay for housing, they live in makeshift shelters. Typically there is no clean water, and their sanitation and energy resources are not adequate. As a result, diseases are rampant, pollution levels keep on rising, and more and more trees are cut down. Some organizations are working with governments to improve sanitation and medical care in megacities.

1. Recognizing Words in Context

Find the word *rampant* in the passage. One definition below is closest to the meaning of that word. One definition has the opposite or nearly opposite meaning. The remaining definition has a completely different meaning. Label the definitions C for *closest*, O for *opposite or nearly opposite*, and D for *different*.

_____ a. uncontrolled

_____ b. restrained

_____ c. random

2. Distinguishing Fact from Opinion

Two of the statements below present *facts*, which can be proved correct. The other statement is an *opinion*, which expresses someone's thoughts or beliefs. Label the statements F for *fact* and O for *opinion*.

_____ a. Megacities are extremely crowded.

_____ b. Some people who live in megacities are wealthy.

_____ c. Fewer people should live in megacities.

3. **Keeping Events in Order**

Label the statements below 1, 2, and 3 to show the order in which the events happen.

_____ a. There are no more trees to cut down.

_____ b. The size of the cities grows and grows.

_____ c. People must go farther and farther to find trees for fuel.

4. **Making Correct Inferences**

Two of the statements below are correct *inferences*, or reasonable guesses. They are based on information in the passage. The other statement is an incorrect, or faulty, inference. Label the statements C for *correct* inference and F for *faulty* inference.

_____ a. An example of a makeshift shelter would be a house made of scrap metal.

_____ b. It is expensive to supply a megacity with clean water.

_____ c. All cities increase in population at the same rate.

5. **Understanding Main Ideas**

One of the statements below expresses the main idea of the passage. One statement is too general, or too broad. The other explains only part of the passage; it is too narrow. Label the statements M for *main idea*, B for *too broad*, and N for *too narrow*.

_____ a. Bombay will soon be the world's largest city.

_____ b. Megacities are the world's largest population centers.

_____ c. City populations are growing faster than rural populations.

Correct Answers, Part A _____

Correct Answers, Part B _____

Total Correct Answers _____

20 A The Relationship of Mathematics to Astronomy and Physics

Although mathematics is not a science, many of its ideas are vital to the various branches of science. Astronomy and physics are especially reliant on math.

From the dawn of civilization, people have studied the movements of planets. Math helped some ancient scientists to predict these movements. As long ago as A.D. 127, the Greek astronomer Ptolemy came up with geometric models for planetary movements. He used these to predict the positions of the Sun, Moon, and planets. He gathered these models in the *Almagest*, a work that was passed on through many cultures. The Muslim astronomer al-Battani used Ptolemy's work to create trigonometric models that could be applied to astronomical computations. His table of co-tangents helped him make accurate observations of the universe.

The *Almagest* was still being used more than a thousand years later by scientists in Europe. In the early 1600s, the German mathematician Johannes Kepler used math to test the heliocentric theory, which stated that the Sun is the center of the universe. This theory contradicted the long-held belief that all heavenly bodies revolved around the planet Earth. Kepler had problems matching the heliocentric theory with the accepted facts. With more effort, he found that the orbits traveled by the planets were ellipses, not circles. He proved this theory with math.

Math is also helpful in physics, even though in ancient times, few physicists used math. Some medieval physicists had discussed applying mathematical descriptions to the actions of falling objects. Still, it was not until the European Renaissance that math was widely held to be a crucial tool for studying the laws of motion. The Italian scientist Galileo applied mathematics to his analysis of how objects fall and projectiles fly. He proved mathematically that, in the absence of air friction, all objects fall at the same speed. This disproved the popular notion that heavy objects fell faster than light ones. The discovery became the basis for the science of mechanics, the study of the actions of force on matter. Galileo also showed that projectiles, such as cannonballs, always moved in a path shaped like an arc, called a parabola.

Another reason math is a good tool for physicists is that it enables them to phrase physical laws. Albert Einstein's theory of relativity is expressed as the algebraic equation $E=mc^2$. Also, many experiments in physics involve measurements. Physicists use math in many ways to develop, expand, and apply new theories.

Reading Time _____

Recalling Facts

1. Al-Battani developed _____ models to describe the movements of heavenly bodies.
   - ❑ a. trigonometric
   - ❑ b. geometric
   - ❑ c. algebraic

2. Which discovery became the basis for the science of mechanics?
   - ❑ a. All objects fall at the same speed.
   - ❑ b. All astral bodies orbit the Sun.
   - ❑ c. All projectiles move in a parabolic path.

3. Ptolemy's astronomical computations helped him to
   - ❑ a. prove the heliocentric theory.
   - ❑ b. predict the position of the Sun.
   - ❑ c. learn about planets' orbits.

4. Before Kepler, astronomers believed that planets moved in
   - ❑ a. a parabolic orbit.
   - ❑ b. a circular orbit.
   - ❑ c. an elliptical orbit.

5. Physicists began using mathematics extensively in their work
   - ❑ a. during medieval times.
   - ❑ b. at the dawn of civilization.
   - ❑ c. during the Renaissance.

Understanding Ideas

6. From the passage, one can conclude that it took a long time for scientists to accurately describe
   - ❑ a. how objects move.
   - ❑ b. the position of planets in the night sky.
   - ❑ c. the speed of falling objects.

7. Which statement represents an accurate conclusion?
   - ❑ a. Ptolemy's *Almagest* was an influential book.
   - ❑ b. Al-Battani revised the *Almagest* to make it better.
   - ❑ c. Galileo could not have discovered how objects fall without the *Almagest*.

8. The medieval period occurred
   - ❑ a. before the time that al-Battani lived.
   - ❑ b. before the time that Ptolemy lived.
   - ❑ c. before the European Renaissance.

9. From reading this article, one can conclude that scientists
   - ❑ a. often draw on the work of earlier scientists.
   - ❑ b. almost always agree on theories.
   - ❑ c. have used mathematics in their work from the beginning of time.

10. Mathematics has enabled physicists and astronomers to
    - ❑ a. learn more about the arts.
    - ❑ b. prove that they are gifted scientists.
    - ❑ c. disprove widely held beliefs.

The scientific method, first introduced in the 1500s, is the process by which scientists perform experiments to prove the laws of nature. The process has evolved over the years, and it now follows a standard series of steps.

The first step is for a person to describe some phenomenon or situation. In the second step, the person states a hypothesis—a proposed explanation for the phenomenon. The hypothesis must be consistent with the person's observations. In the third step, the person uses this hypothesis to make a prediction. For the last step, the person tests this explanation by doing experiments or making further observations. If the results of the experiments or observations support the hypothesis, it becomes a theory. If the results do not support the hypothesis, then it may be rejected or modified in light of the results. Any new or changed hypotheses must be tested again, using all the steps described above. Just as before, the new hypothesis can become a theory only if the experiments or observations prove it.

It is important for the person to remain completely objective when using the scientific method, even if the person has strong feelings about the correctness of the hypothesis. He or she must not allow his or her emotions to affect the way the experiment is conducted or interpreted. The observer must make all observations and regard all data without bias.

1. **Recognizing Words in Context**

    Find the word *bias* in the passage. One definition below is closest to the meaning of that word. One definition has the opposite or nearly opposite meaning. The remaining definition has a completely different meaning. Label the definitions C for *closest*, O for *opposite or nearly opposite*, and D for *different*.

    _____ a. carelessness

    _____ b. objectivity

    _____ c. prejudice

2. **Distinguishing Fact from Opinion**

    Two of the statements below present *facts*, which can be proved correct. The other statement is an *opinion*, which expresses someone's thoughts or beliefs. Label the statements F for *fact* and O for *opinion*.

    _____ a. The scientific method has led to important discoveries in science.

    _____ b. The scientific method has evolved over many years.

    _____ c. The scientific method is one of the best ways of proving a hypothesis.

3. Keeping Events in Order

Label the statements below 1, 2, and 3 to show the order in which the events happen.

_____ a. A person conducts an experiment.

_____ b. A person states a hypothesis.

_____ c. A person describes a phenomenon.

4. Making Correct Inferences

Two of the statements below are correct *inferences,* or reasonable guesses. They are based on information in the passage. The other statement is an incorrect, or faulty, inference. Label the statements C for *correct* inference and F for *faulty* inference.

_____ a. The scientific method can be a lengthy process.

_____ b. Good theories are based on accurate experiments or observations.

_____ c. A good experiment will always prove a hypothesis to be correct.

5. Understanding Main Ideas

One of the statements below expresses the main idea of the passage. One statement is too general, or too broad. The other explains only part of the passage; it is too narrow. Label the statements M for *main idea,* B for *too broad,* and N for *too narrow.*

_____ a. Scientists have come up with standard ways of doing their work.

_____ b. The scientific method is a series of steps that helps prove the laws of nature.

_____ c. Stating a hypothesis is an important part of the scientific process.

Correct Answers, Part A _____

Correct Answers, Part B _____

Total Correct Answers _____

Weather Forecasting Tools

Meteorologists are scientists who study the weather and make weather forecasts. Most people know that a weather thermometer measures air temperature, but they may not know about the other tools that meteorologists use.

Barometers measure the air pressure in the atmosphere. One type of barometer is the mercury barometer. When the liquid in the device steadily drops, it usually indicates the approach of a storm. When the mercury is on the rise, good weather is probably on its way. The aneroid barometer has no liquid. Instead, it is an airtight box. The sides of the box move in and out according to the amount of air pressure.

Radar is used to gather information about clouds and rain. It can track the direction of precipitation. It can also tell the difference between the tiny raindrops of a normal cloud and the large ones that mark a bad storm.

Meteorologists use anemometers to measure wind speed and direction. The most common type of anemometer for finding wind speed is the revolving-cup electric anemometer. This device is somewhat like a pinwheel. Cups mounted on a rod are spun around by the wind, making the rod turn. The rod is connected to an electric generator that measures how many times the cups go around in a set amount of time. Wind speed and direction are also measured by a newer type of radar called Doppler radar. It allows meteorologists to measure the speed and direction of windblown precipitation. With Doppler radar, they can see when and where severe thunderstorms and tornadoes are forming.

Humidity—the amount of water vapor in the air—is measured by hygrometers. The psychrometer is the most common type used. It is made of two thermometers: one gives the real temperature, and the other is kept wet. The psychrometer is spun so that water evaporates from the wet thermometer—in high humidity, less water will evaporate. The difference between the temperature readings taken from these two thermometers is checked against data tables that provide humidity readings.

Radiosonde balloons have instruments that gather readings for temperature, pressure, humidity, and wind. The data are fed into computers that can calculate how weather systems are moving and predict how they might change.

Satellites that orbit Earth also take temperature and moisture readings. In addition, they take pictures of cloud formations. Computer programs analyze these pictures to compute the speeds of wind and storms.

Reading Time _____

Recalling Facts

1. A psychrometer is composed of two thermometers because
   - ❏ a. the difference between the two temperatures of the two thermometers helps determine humidity.
   - ❏ b. one thermometer measures the inside temperature while the other measures the outside temperature.
   - ❏ c. if one thermometer breaks while it is spinning, the other can give the reading.

2. The difference between the mercury and aneroid barometer is that
   - ❏ a. one has liquid, and the other doesn't.
   - ❏ b. one measures rising air pressure, and the other measures dropping air pressure.
   - ❏ c. one reacts to air pressure outside, and the other reacts to air pressure indoors.

3. Doppler radar measures wind speed and direction by creating images of
   - ❏ a. satellite pictures.
   - ❏ b. humidity and air pressure.
   - ❏ c. precipitation blown by wind.

4. An anemometer measures
   - ❏ a. the amount of precipitation.
   - ❏ b. wind speed and direction.
   - ❏ c. relative humidity.

5. Radiosonde balloons and satellites provide data that are
   - ❏ a. most useful for forecasting snow.
   - ❏ b. similar to information provided by radar.
   - ❏ c. analyzed by computers.

Understanding Ideas

6. The article suggests that more sophisticated forecast tools have resulted in
   - ❏ a. more accurate weather predictions.
   - ❏ b. the replacement of basic devices like thermometers.
   - ❏ c. the replacement of nearly all meteorologists by computers.

7. Radar would be most useful for
   - ❏ a. measuring wind speed.
   - ❏ b. identifying storm clouds.
   - ❏ c. tracking changes in air pressure.

8. A fall in the mercury level in a mercury barometer would most likely show that
   - ❏ a. rain is approaching.
   - ❏ b. clear skies are approaching.
   - ❏ c. the humidity is decreasing.

9. From the passage, you can infer that a radiosonde balloon is a useful tool for forecasters because it
   - ❏ a. is controlled by a computer.
   - ❏ b. analyzes cloud movements and calculates wind speed.
   - ❏ c. collects different types of data.

10. Weather forecasters are interested in wind direction because it can
    - ❏ a. determine where tornadoes will hit.
    - ❏ b. help them predict the kind of weather and where it is headed.
    - ❏ c. help them predict weather systems up to two weeks in advance.

Making a Hygrometer

By assembling a few simple materials, you can make a hygrometer that shows the relative humidity. The materials required are one cardboard milk carton, scissors, a shoelace with both ends cut off, two identical outdoor thermometers, a piece of string, two rubber bands, a glass of water, and a piece of cardboard. It is a good idea to have an adult help you construct the device.

First, cut the top off the milk carton, forming a rectangular box. Second, wrap one end of the shoelace around the bulb of one of the thermometers, tie the end firmly in place with a piece of string, and make sure that the shoelace completely covers the bulb. Third, attach both thermometers to the outside of the milk carton with the rubber bands. Fourth, cut a small slit into the carton right below the thermometer with the shoelace, and thread the shoelace's other end through this hole. Finally, add water to the milk carton up to the slit, making sure that the shoelace is completely immersed. The shoelace will slowly absorb the water until the section around the thermometer bulb is damp.

Put your hygrometer someplace where it will not be disturbed. After several days, use the cardboard to fan the hygrometer for 15 seconds or so. Then take temperature readings from each thermometer and record the readings. Using the Internet, locate a relative humidity chart for hygrometers and calculate the humidity.

1. **Recognizing Words in Context**

   Find the word *immersed* in the passage. One definition below is closest to the meaning of that word. One definition has the opposite or nearly opposite meaning. The remaining definition has a completely different meaning. Label the definitions C for *closest*, O for *opposite or nearly opposite*, and D for *different*.

   _____ a. above water

   _____ b. underwater

   _____ c. without water

2. **Distinguishing Fact from Opinion**

   Two of the statements below present *facts*, which can be proved correct. The other statement is an *opinion*, which expresses someone's thoughts or beliefs. Label the statements F for *fact* and O for *opinion*.

   _____ a. To provide accurate readings, a hygrometer should be left undisturbed.

   _____ b. Making a hygrometer is simple.

   _____ c. A conversion chart is needed to figure out the relative humidity.

3. Keeping Events in Order

Label the statements below 1, 2, and 3 to show the order in which the steps should be completed.

_____ a. Tie the shoelace over the bulb with a string.

_____ b. Put the shoelace through the carton's slit.

_____ c. Make sure that the shoelace completely covers the bulb.

4. Making Correct Inferences

Two of the statements below are correct *inferences*, or reasonable guesses. They are based on information in the passage. The other statement is an incorrect, or faulty, inference. Label the statements C for *correct* inference and F for *faulty* inference.

_____ a. A homemade hygrometer is the best tool for determining relative humidity in the air.

_____ b. This experiment cannot be completed in one day.

_____ c. It is important to be careful when performing science experiments.

5. Understanding Main Ideas

One of the statements below expresses the main idea of the passage. One statement is too general, or too broad. The other explains only part of the passage; it is too narrow. Label the statements M for *main idea*, B for *too broad*, and N for *too narrow*.

_____ a. A hygrometer can be assembled by using a few simple materials.

_____ b. A hygrometer is a device that helps to measure humidity in the air.

_____ c. A special chart is needed to figure out relative humidity.

Correct Answers, Part A _____

Correct Answers, Part B _____

Total Correct Answers _____

The Machine Age in the United States

The Machine Age was a period in U.S. history that was typified by enormous growth in the use of machines at both work and home. The Machine Age began in about 1900 and hit its peak in the 1920s.

The growing availability of electricity was perhaps the most important development of the Machine Age. Vast networks of power lines appeared in cities for the first time. As electricity became cheap and plentiful, the use of electricity multiplied a thousandfold in only a few years. Americans soon had more than 50 newly invented electrical home appliances to choose from, including vacuum cleaners, washing machines, electric stoves, and refrigerators. New technology also provided new forms of entertainment. In large numbers, people in the United States began to frequently go to the "moving pictures," or movies. They also listened to programs on the radio, and they chatted on the telephone.

The growth of the automobile industry greatly changed life for many Americans. Carmaker Henry Ford wanted to produce a car that was affordable to the average American. Through mass production, he was able to make cars more quickly than people had thought possible; in 1912, a Ford factory could assemble a car in just two hours. By the end of the decade, Ford was selling more than 1 million cars annually.

Ford achieved mass production in his factories by using assembly lines. His assembly line was a system of chains, slides, and conveyors that moved parts of a product from one worker to another. Each automotive worker performed only one task, such as driving tacks into a seat cushion. Not only did many workers find this new method of work dull, but they also had to work very quickly to keep up with the pace of the assembly line. For some workers, the assembly line illustrated the notion that people themselves were becoming little more than machine parts. This idea was perhaps best seen in the German film *Metropolis,* which appeared in 1926. It showed a city of the future where the workers are forced to stay underground, running the machinery that runs the world above them.

Still, most Americans embraced the new forms of technology, appreciating the conveniences and jobs that were added to society. Indeed, the Machine Age had a strong influence on American culture. For example, art forms such as painting and photography began to make use of the symbolism of machinery.

Reading Time _____

Recalling Facts

1. The Machine Age began with the
   - ❑ a. use of the assembly line.
   - ❑ b. emergence of many new technologies.
   - ❑ c. movie *Metropolis.*

2. The word _____ does *not* characterize work on the assembly line.
   - ❑ a. repetitive
   - ❑ b. creative
   - ❑ c. hectic

3. According to the article, what was probably the most important technology of the Machine Age?
   - ❑ a. "moving pictures"
   - ❑ b. the automobile
   - ❑ c. electricity

4. Americans reacted to new forms of entertainment by
   - ❑ a. enjoying them often.
   - ❑ b. thinking that they were too difficult to use.
   - ❑ c. protesting.

5. Ford's goal was to
   - ❑ a. sell more cars than anyone else.
   - ❑ b. make a car that most people could afford.
   - ❑ c. produce the fastest car in the world.

Understanding Ideas

6. The Machine Age got its name because
   - ❑ a. new machinery influenced all aspects of life.
   - ❑ b. Americans created artistic crafts with their new machinery.
   - ❑ c. machinery began to run the workplaces.

7. It is possible to conclude from the article that work for housewives improved during the Machine Age because they were able to
   - ❑ a. mimic assembly-line techniques.
   - ❑ b. cook more meals per day.
   - ❑ c. use many labor-saving devices.

8. Car ownership had risen by the 1920s because
   - ❑ a. car factories employed many people.
   - ❑ b. car prices were more affordable.
   - ❑ c. cars were necessary in order for people to get to work.

9. According to the article, how did the majority of Americans feel about these modern times?
   - ❑ a. positive
   - ❑ b. alarmed
   - ❑ c. uninterested

10. The maker of the film *Metropolis* would probably agree that
    - ❑ a. machinery does a better job than humans.
    - ❑ b. the city of the future will be a better place.
    - ❑ c. workers in the Machine Age were mistreated.

Nutcrackers, axes, wells, and wheelbarrows all share one extremely fundamental similarity: They are simple machines that were found around many homes before and during the Machine Age. A simple machine is one of the most rudimentary devices for doing work.

A nutcracker is an example of a lever, which is a machine that allows a person to use a minimum amount of effort to move a maximum load. Think about the nutcracker. Effort—the motion of closing the handles—is applied to one part of the lever; this lever pushes a load—the nut—at its other end. The lever acts as a force magnifier, so the effort is enough to crack open the hard shell of the nut.

An ax is a simple machine known as a wedge. When an ax is swung at firewood or at a tree, the force of the effort drives the thinner end of the ax blade into the wood, severing the wood.

A wheel on an axle is used to bring water from the depths of a well. A rope is fastened around the axle, customarily a bar, and attached to the load, a bucket. When the handle on the wheel is turned to rotate the axle, the bucket is lowered into the well.

A wheelbarrow is a combination of two simple machines: the lever and the wheel on an axle. A person can transport heavy objects with a wheelbarrow because it functions as a lever, and the wheel makes it easier to move the object from place to place.

1. Recognizing Words in Context

Find the word *rudimentary* in the passage. One definition below is closest to the meaning of that word. One definition has the opposite or nearly opposite meaning. The remaining definition has a completely different meaning. Label the definitions C for *closest*, O for *opposite or nearly opposite*, and D for *different*.

_____ a. complex

_____ b. basic

_____ c. useful

2. Distinguishing Fact from Opinion

Two of the statements below present *facts*, which can be proved correct. The other statement is an *opinion*, which expresses someone's thoughts or beliefs. Label the statements F for *fact* and O for *opinion*.

_____ a. A wedge is a simple machine that people use to cut wood.

_____ b. People should use wheelbarrows when moving heavy objects in the yard.

_____ c. Some tools combine different simple machines.

3. Keeping Events in Order

Label the statements below 1, 2, and 3 to show the order in which the events happen.

_____ a. Effort is applied to one part of the nutcracker.

_____ b. The nutcracker pushes the load at its other end.

_____ c. The nut cracks open.

4. Making Correct Inferences

Two of the statements below are correct *inferences,* or reasonable guesses. They are based on information in the passage. The other statement is an incorrect, or faulty, inference. Label the statements C for *correct* inference and F for *faulty* inference.

_____ a. Many people are unaware of the simple machines they use on a regular basis.

_____ b. The lever can move larger loads than other types of simple machines.

_____ c. An axle is any object that revolves.

5. Understanding Main Ideas

One of the statements below expresses the main idea of the passage. One statement is too general, or too broad. The other explains only part of the passage; it is too narrow. Label the statements M for *main idea,* B for *too broad,* and N for *too narrow.*

_____ a. Simple machines perform work in and around the home.

_____ b. The lever is a simple machine found in many homes.

_____ c. Some machines are complex, and some are very simple.

Correct Answers, Part A _____

Correct Answers, Part B _____

Total Correct Answers _____

The "space race" took place between the United States and the former
Soviet Union. Both countries competed to see which would be the first to
land a person on the Moon.

Early space ventures were limited to satellites that orbited the planet
Earth. The Soviets launched the world's first satellite on October 4, 1957;
Sputnik I orbited Earth more than a thousand times before it plunged back
into the planet's atmosphere and burned up. The United States' first satellite
was *Explorer 1*, launched the following January.

In 1959, both the United States and the Soviet Union succeeded in
achieving their goal of sending spacecraft called probes beyond Earth's
gravitational pull. The Soviet *Luna I*, launched on January 2, passed the
Moon and continued through space. Two months later, the United States
launched *Pioneer 4*, which followed the same path as *Luna*. Both probes
eventually entered orbit around the Sun.

The first person in space was Soviet cosmonaut Yuri Gagarin. He orbited
Earth in *Vostok I* on April 12, 1961. The United States began to catch up
in the race by sending Alan Shepard into space in *Freedom 7* on May 5,
1961. The following February, John Glenn became the first American to
orbit Earth.

Over the next seven years, both the Americans and the Soviets sent many
astronauts into space. The most famous was U.S. astronaut Neil Armstrong,
who, on July 20, 1969, became the first human to set foot on the Moon.
The United States Apollo program lasted until 1972; its missions carried
out extensive research of the lunar surface and even brought back samples
of moon rocks.

The history of space exploration also has seen men and women living
on space stations. The Soviets sent the first such station into space in 1971.
The first U.S. space station, *Skylab*, was launched in May 1973 and orbited
for six years. Since the 1960s, both countries also have sent spacecraft to
explore almost all the planets in the solar system. Atmospheric probes, surface
landings, and flybys have produced photographs of and information about
the surfaces, moons, and atmospheres of many planets. However, humans
have not yet set foot on any other planet.

Space exploration has helped countries develop new technologies. It also
has helped scientists gain a better understanding of the universe. Future
space missions may help them answer some of the basic questions about the
origin of matter.

Reading Time _____

Recalling Facts

1. The first goal of both the U.S. and Soviet space programs was to
   - ❏ a. put a satellite in orbit.
   - ❏ b. land a person on the Moon.
   - ❏ c. build a space station.

2. Yuri Gagarin is famous because he was the first person to
   - ❏ a. travel in space.
   - ❏ b. set foot on the Moon.
   - ❏ c. explore another planet.

3. A cosmonaut is a
   - ❏ a. satellite.
   - ❏ b. Soviet astronaut.
   - ❏ c. type of spacecraft.

4. Spacecraft have traveled to _____ the planets.
   - ❏ a. most of
   - ❏ b. few of
   - ❏ c. all of

5. The first satellites
   - ❏ a. studied the Moon.
   - ❏ b. orbited Earth.
   - ❏ c. took photographs of other planets.

Understanding Ideas

6. Which statement is probably true about the Apollo program?
   - ❏ a. It was considered a success.
   - ❏ b. It was deemed too dangerous.
   - ❏ c. It studied the planets nearest to Earth.

7. The prime aim of the U.S. space program continues to be to
   - ❏ a. send a spacecraft in orbit around the Sun.
   - ❏ b. send people to live in space.
   - ❏ c. learn more about the galaxy.

8. One can conclude that the 1969 Moon landing was historic because it
   - ❏ a. was the first manned space mission.
   - ❏ b. brought moon samples to scientists.
   - ❏ c. put the first human on a heavenly body.

9. From the article, one can infer that
   - ❏ a. steady progress has been maintained since space exploration first began.
   - ❏ b. the United States gradually became less and less interested in space exploration over time.
   - ❏ c. the Soviets have been much less accomplished in space exploration than the Americans.

10. One can infer that the United States and the Soviet Union each wanted to win the "space race" to
    - ❏ a. obtain valuable Moon rocks.
    - ❏ b. appear superior in comparison to its competitor.
    - ❏ c. create a colony on the Moon.

Space scientists, mathematicians, and physicists are members of the National Aeronautics and Space Administration (NASA) ground crew that is crucial to keeping spacecraft on course. Tracking teams are needed to compute the paths of spacecraft in Earth's orbit and in deep space. Katherine Johnson was a pioneer in this field and worked in it for 30 years. Her algebraic equations, which she derived using just pencil and paper, helped chart the proper courses for spacecraft. Navigation from Earth to space and back is difficult, because Earth is constantly in motion around the Sun. Travel to the Moon is even more difficult, because the Moon moves differently than Earth does.

In addition to mathematical equations, radar greatly helps the work of tracking teams. Tracking stations on Earth send radio waves into deep space. When these beams bounce off of the spacecraft, the trackers analyze the returned signals. Then they compare this data to computer models that show where the probe would be traveling, assuming a certain starting position. This comparison allows trackers to make the best guess regarding the spacecraft's position. Satellites that are traveling close to Earth can be tracked by radio signals or by telescope cameras.

NASA runs 14 tracking stations. Of these, 3 are part of the deep-space network, which means that they can track vehicles deep into space.

1. **Recognizing Words in Context**

   Find the word *derived* in the passage. One definition below is closest to the meaning of that word. One definition has the opposite or nearly opposite meaning. The remaining definition has a completely different meaning. Label the definitions C for *closest*, O for *opposite or nearly opposite*, and D for *different*.

   _____ a. created

   _____ b. erased

   _____ c. solved

2. **Distinguishing Fact from Opinion**

   Two of the statements below present *facts*, which can be proved correct. The other statement is an *opinion*, which expresses someone's thoughts or beliefs. Label the statements F for *fact* and O for *opinion*.

   _____ a. Trackers use telescope cameras to follow satellites.

   _____ b. Katherine Johnson made important calculations dealing with space navigation.

   _____ c. Space trackers have an interesting and challenging job.

3. **Keeping Events in Order**

Label the statements below 1, 2, and 3 to show the order in which the events happen.

_____ a. Tracking stations send radio signals into space.

_____ b. Trackers estimate the spacecraft's position.

_____ c. Radar signals bounce off the spacecraft.

4. **Making Correct Inferences**

Two of the statements below are correct *inferences,* or reasonable guesses. They are based on information in the passage. The other statement is an incorrect, or faulty, inference. Label the statements C for *correct* inference and F for *faulty* inference.

_____ a. A knowledge of algebra is the most important requirement for a space tracker.

_____ b. The work of space trackers is crucial to maintaining the safety of astronauts.

_____ c. Space trackers have a challenging job.

5. **Understanding Main Ideas**

One of the statements below expresses the main idea of the passage. One statement is too general, or too broad. The other explains only part of the passage; it is too narrow. Label the statements M for *main idea,* B for *too broad,* and N for *too narrow.*

_____ a. Space trackers such as Johnson have used radar and math to help spacecraft stay on course.

_____ b. NASA runs three deep-space tracking stations.

_____ c. Tracking stations on Earth follow spacecraft traveling in outer space.

Correct Answers, Part A _____

Correct Answers, Part B _____

Total Correct Answers _____

Television is defined as the transmission of pictures over distances. The first step in the invention of television dates back to 1883, when Paul Nipkow invented a scanning disk in Germany. Nipkow pierced a metal disk with a single row of holes that spiraled inward to the middle of the disk. Nipkow used a disk for transmitting and another for receiving. The transmitting disk revolved in front of a plate upon which an image was placed. In one turn, the disk scanned the entire image. The plate was connected to an electric circuit that picked up and carried the variations in light produced by the image. The receiving disk picked up the current and then reproduced the picture on another plate.

Nipkow's system used wires to transmit images. With the appearance of wireless radio in the early 1900s, inventors worked on television systems that could transmit through the air. These inventors captured pictures, coded them by radio waves, and transformed them into images on a screen. In 1926 two inventors, one in the United States and one in Great Britain, used scanning disks in wireless transmission systems.

Around the same time, however, two other inventors working in the United States, Vladimir K. Zworykin and Philo T. Farnsworth, made key contributions with their electronic television systems. These systems used cathode ray tubes—specialized electrical devices for showing images—in place of the mechanical scanning disks.

In 1923 Zworykin had introduced the iconoscope, the first truly successful camera tube. A scanner passing across the surface of a television camera tube picks up the varying light intensities of an image and converts the image into electric signals. At the same time, the scanner beams these signals onto a screen, where the image appears.

Farnsworth came up with the idea of scanning lines of electron beams and magnetically deflecting them so that together the lines would form a moving picture. After several years of working on this venture, Farnsworth built a television camera tube that scanned images line by line. Farnsworth demonstrated the first electronic television image—a straight line—in San Francisco on September 7, 1927.

Despite these advances, the development of television still had a long road ahead. Although both Zworykin and Farnsworth obtained major financial backing and continued to work on their systems, television was not introduced to mass audiences until 1939 at the World's Fair in New York City.

Reading Time _____

Recalling Facts

1. Which of these inventors did not contribute to the development of electronic television?
   - ❑ a. Vladimir K. Zworykin
   - ❑ b. Samuel Morse
   - ❑ c. Philo T. Farnsworth

2. The scanning disk was invented in
   - ❑ a. Great Britain.
   - ❑ b. San Francisco.
   - ❑ c. Germany.

3. The first successful camera tube was introduced in
   - ❑ c. 1923.
   - ❑ b. 1926.
   - ❑ c. 1927.

4. The first electronic television image was of
   - ❑ a. the World's Fair.
   - ❑ b. a radio.
   - ❑ c. a straight line.

5. Farnsworth's camera tube scanned an image
   - ❑ a. in a circle.
   - ❑ b. line by line.
   - ❑ c. mechanically.

Understanding Ideas

6. From the article, it is possible to conclude that the development of television was
   - ❑ a. a lengthy process.
   - ❑ b. difficult but rapid.
   - ❑ c. the work of one person.

7. Television could not work without
   - ❑ a. scanning disks.
   - ❑ b. wire transmitters.
   - ❑ c. electrical signals.

8. According to the article, how did cathode ray tubes compare with scanning disks?
   - ❑ a. Cathode ray tubes were better.
   - ❑ b. Cathode ray tubes were more expensive.
   - ❑ c. Cathode ray tubes were older.

9. Farnsworth and Zworykin probably
   - ❑ a. stole each other's ideas.
   - ❑ b. were competitors.
   - ❑ c. lived in Great Britain.

10. One of the things that can be learned from the article is that
    - ❑ a. most people didn't believe television would work.
    - ❑ b. several inventors contributed to the development of television.
    - ❑ c. people debated whether mechanical television or electronic television was better.

The television of the future will bring a great deal of change in quality, quantity, and variety. One big change will be high-definition television, or HDTV. The United States plans to adopt this system within a few years, and HDTV broadcasting has already begun. The system uses digital signals, providing sharper, clearer images and sound. With a wide-screen picture and stereo surround-sound, this type of television will provide an experience similar to going to the movies.

In the future, computers, the Internet, and television will likely be linked more closely than they are today. Some stations are now trying out interactive television. This allows the viewer to participate in TV programs via the Internet. Before the Internet, the only way to interact with a TV show was by calling in to a live program. Now viewers can use interactive television to participate in instant opinion polls, to shop at home, or to compete in game shows.

Television on demand may be a wave of the future as well. Today's TV schedule could be superseded by a system that lets viewers watch or store programs whenever they want. Even now, some TV systems allow viewers to record and store multiple programs. This means that viewers can watch shows according to their own schedules, not those of the TV stations. The new TV will also have multicasting, in which one station can broadcast many channels, all with different programs.

1. **Recognizing Words in Context**

   Find the word *superseded* in the passage. One definition below is closest to the meaning of that word. One definition has the opposite or nearly opposite meaning. The remaining definition has a completely different meaning. Label the definitions C for *closest*, O for *opposite or nearly opposite*, and D for *different*.

   _____ a. replaced

   _____ b. grown

   _____ c. introduced

2. **Distinguishing Fact from Opinion**

   Two of the statements below present *facts*, which can be proved correct. The other statement is an *opinion*, which expresses someone's thoughts or beliefs. Label the statements F for *fact* and O for *opinion*.

   _____ a. Interactive television is being used today.

   _____ b. Television on demand allows viewers to choose their own programming.

   _____ c. Watching television is becoming more and more enriching.

3. Keeping Events in Order

Label the statements below 1, 2, and 3 to show the order in which the events can happen.

_____ a. Interactive television is introduced.

_____ b. TV broadcasters begin working with Internet companies.

_____ c. The Internet is introduced.

4. Making Correct Inferences

Two of the statements below are correct *inferences*, or reasonable guesses. They are based on information in the passage. The other statement is an incorrect, or faulty, inference. Label the statements C for *correct* inference and F for *faulty* inference.

_____ a. TV technology will continue to improve.

_____ b. In the future, TV programming will consist mainly of movies.

_____ c. The Internet has played a part in changes made to television.

5. Understanding Main Ideas

One of the statements below expresses the main idea of the passage. One statement is too general, or too broad. The other explains only part of the passage; it is too narrow. Label the statements M for *main idea,* B for *too broad,* and N for *too narrow.*

_____ a. Advances in television will provide more choices and better quality pictures.

_____ b. Some stations are using interactive television.

_____ c. Television is one of the most popular forms of entertainment.

Correct Answers, Part A _____

Correct Answers, Part B _____

Total Correct Answers _____

Scientists study the ocean in many different ways. Although many marine scientists focus on animals in the ocean, others seek to gain a better understanding of the ocean's chemical and physical components. Scientists are learning a great deal about the natural and human-induced processes that shape the ocean and its many life forms.

Much of the current research focuses on how human activity affects the ocean. Clean water is a limited resource, and ocean pollution endangers plant and animal health. Some scientists are currently analyzing ocean water to find out just how contaminated it is. Scientists are also working on new methods to evaluate the presence of toxins in the ocean, which will help them develop better techniques for cleaning up the water. Others look at how sea organisms adapt to exposure to toxins. Toxic sea life has an effect on humans too. For example, some mussels metabolize, or break down, toxins in their tissues, which may pose a threat to humans who eat the mussels.

Another type of marine scientist strives to learn more about the history of the ocean. Understanding the ocean's past tells scientists more about its patterns and cycles today and in the future. The ocean's past, which is recorded by deposits in the ocean floor, helps scientists understand such crucial issues as global climate change and other environmental variations. The more researchers learn about the history of the ocean and its relation to climatic and environmental changes, the more likely that they will one day understand what causes such changes.

Other scientists are concerned with understanding how ocean systems work. The word *systems* refers to all the conditions and elements that are continually changing the ocean. Comprehending these systems is necessary to protect the ocean and ensure the safety of its life forms. The cycles of ocean life also have an enormous effect on human life; for example, studying coastal waters is important because they provide much of the fish that humans consume.

Marine geologists are earth scientists who work along the ocean floor. The Ocean Drilling Program, a 20-nation effort, drills the ocean floor and removes material for study. Among other accomplishments, this program has found evidence of a giant meteorite impact, which supports the theory that dinosaurs became extinct after Earth underwent a climate change caused by a collision with a large meteor. Other marine geologists focus on more current events, such as the erosion of shorelines.

Reading Time _____

Recalling Facts

1. The Ocean Drilling Program
   - ❏ a. is based in the United States.
   - ❏ b. is an international organization.
   - ❏ c. studies only past events.

2. Some scientists study the relationship between the history of the ocean and
   - ❏ a. the changes in the ocean's climate and environment.
   - ❏ b. the feeding habits of dinosaurs.
   - ❏ c. the rate at which people consume mussels.

3. _____ might have caused the extinction of the dinosaurs.
   - ❏ a. Water pollution
   - ❏ b. Exposure to toxins
   - ❏ c. A climate change resulting from a meteorite crash

4. Coastal waters are important to human life because they
   - ❏ a. are the most contaminated.
   - ❏ b. indicate climatic change.
   - ❏ c. provide much of the fish that people eat.

5. Techniques to clean up ocean water draw upon
   - ❏ a. how many organisms live in the water.
   - ❏ b. how polluted the water is.
   - ❏ c. how ocean systems work.

Understanding Ideas

6. If humans eat animals that are toxic, they will likely
   - ❏ a. feel no effect.
   - ❏ b. be harmed.
   - ❏ c. become immune to that toxin.

7. From the article, you can infer that one focus of marine geology is
   - ❏ a. coastal erosion.
   - ❏ b. the history of the ocean.
   - ❏ c. the development of sea organisms.

8. The article seems to indicate that the most serious harm currently done to the ocean is caused by
   - ❏ a. human activity.
   - ❏ b. meteorites.
   - ❏ c. natural toxins.

9. In what way do marine geologists compare with other marine scientists?
   - ❏ a. They perform their research on the floor of the ocean.
   - ❏ b. They seek to learn more about the ocean's history.
   - ❏ c. They focus their work on ocean pollution.

10. One thing you can learn from the article is that
   - ❏ a. the ocean poses many dangers.
   - ❏ b. scientists can learn a great deal from studying the ocean.
   - ❏ c. almost all marine scientists study animal life.

The Future of the Ocean

Just a few years ago, scientists discovered previously unknown types of life that survive at deep ocean depths. Instead of drawing energy from the sun, these life forms draw energy from chemicals under the sea floor. Such new findings show why an understanding of the ocean is crucial to protecting it.

As part of the drive to protect the ocean, environmentalists named 1998 as "Year of the Ocean." That June, President Clinton met with scientists, environmentalists, and others to discuss the future of the ocean. The next year, the U.S. government issued a report that said protecting the ocean and coastal areas was not optional but, rather, imperative.

The report urged that action be taken to ensure the survival of endangered marine life. Recently, the United States developed a system to protect the 300 remaining North Atlantic right whales. A ship entering the whales' feeding and nursing grounds off Cape Cod in Massachusetts now must report details about its route and speed to the U.S. Coast Guard. This helps prevent collisions between ships and whales.

The report also recommended that stronger efforts be made to keep the oceans clean. Current studies show that such ocean debris as soda cans, plastic bags, and cigarette butts threatens more than 200 species of marine and coastal wildlife. Citizens can help in this effort. In 1998, nearly 160,000 volunteers removed about 3.3 million pounds of garbage from U.S. shorelines.

1. Recognizing Words in Context

Find the word *imperative* in the passage. One definition below is closest to the meaning of that word. One definition has the opposite or nearly opposite meaning. The remaining definition has a completely different meaning. Label the definitions C for *closest*, O for *opposite or nearly opposite*, and D for *different*.

_____ a. nonessential

_____ b. essential

_____ c. experiment

2. Distinguishing Fact from Opinion

Two of the statements below present *facts*, which can be proved correct. The other statement is an *opinion*, which expresses someone's thoughts or beliefs. Label the statements F for *fact* and O for *opinion*.

_____ a. Ships around Cape Cod report their movements to the U.S. Coast Guard.

_____ b. There are life forms that can survive on the floor of the ocean.

_____ c. People should spend more time learning about the ocean.

3. Keeping Events in Order

Label the statements below 1, 2, and 3 to show the order in which the events happen.

_____ a. The United States issues a report about protecting the ocean.

_____ b. The "Year of the Ocean" is declared.

_____ c. Scientists and environmentalists meet to discuss the future of the ocean.

4. Making Correct Inferences

Two of the statements below are correct *inferences,* or reasonable guesses. They are based on information in the passage. The other statement is an incorrect, or faulty, inference. Label the statements C for *correct* inference and F for *faulty* inference.

_____ a. Many countries can contribute to ocean preservation.

_____ b. If scientists work hard, all species facing extinction can be saved.

_____ c. The North Atlantic right whale population is safer now.

5. Understanding Main Ideas

One of the statements below expresses the main idea of the passage. One statement is too general, or too broad. The other explains only part of the passage; it is too narrow. Label the statements M for *main idea,* B for *too broad,* and N for *too narrow.*

_____ a. More efforts are needed to study and protect the ocean.

_____ b. The Year of the Ocean took place in 1998.

_____ c. Oceans are an important part of Earth's ecology.

Correct Answers, Part A _____

Correct Answers, Part B _____

Total Correct Answers _____

ANSWER KEY

READING RATE GRAPH

COMPREHENSION SCORE GRAPH

COMPREHENSION SKILLS PROFILE GRAPH

ANSWER KEY

1A	1. b	2. b	3. c	4. a	5. b	6. a	7. c	8. c	9. b	10. a
1B	1. D, O, C	2. O, F, F	3. 3, 1, 2	4. F, C, C	5. B, M, N					
2A	1. a	2. c	3. a	4. b	5. a	6. c	7. b	8. a	9. b	10. c
2B	1. O, D, C	2. F, F, O	3. 3, 1, 2	4. C, C, F	5. N, M, B					
3A	1. a	2. a	3. c	4. c	5. a	6. a	7. c	8. b	9. c	10. c
3B	1. O, C, D	2. F, O, F	3. 2, 1, 3	4. F, C, C	5. M, B, N					
4A	1. c	2. a	3. c	4. a	5. a	6. b	7. c	8. b	9. b	10. c
4B	1. D, O, C	2. O, F, F	3. 3, 2, 1	4. C, F, C	5. B, N, M					
5A	1. b	2. b	3. a	4. c	5. b	6. a	7. b	8. c	9. b	10. a
5B	1. C, O, D	2. F, O, F	3. 3, 2, 1	4. C, C, F	5. N, B, M					
6A	1. c	2. b	3. c	4. a	5. a	6. c	7. b	8. c	9. a	10. c
6B	1. C, D, O	2. F, O, F	3. 3, 2, 1	4. F, C, C	5. B, N, M					
7A	1. a	2. b	3. c	4. a	5. c	6. a	7. b	8. c	9. c	10. b
7B	1. D, O, C	2. F, F, O	3. 3, 1, 2	4. C, F, C	5. B, M, N					
8A	1. c	2. a	3. b	4. c	5. b	6. a	7. a	8. c	9. b	10. c
8B	1. O, C, D	2. F, O, F	3. 1, 3, 2	4. C, F, C	5. B, N, M					
9A	1. b	2. a	3. c	4. a	5. b	6. b	7. a	8. b	9. c	10. c
9B	1. D, C, O	2. O, F, F	3. 1, 3, 2	4. C, C, F	5. N, M, B					
10A	1. a	2. b	3. c	4. c	5. b	6. b	7. a	8. b	9. c	10. a
10B	1. C, D, O	2. O, F, F	3. 2, 1, 3	4. C, C, F	5. B, N, M					
11A	1. b	2. a	3. b	4. b	5. c	6. b	7. a	8. b	9. c	10. b
11B	1. O, C, D	2. F, F, O	3. 2, 3, 1	4. C, C, F	5. N, M, B					
12A	1. c	2. b	3. a	4. b	5. c	6. a	7. b	8. a	9. b	10. c
12B	1. O, C, D	2. F, F, O	3. 1, 3, 2	4. C, C, F	5. M, N, B					
13A	1. a	2. c	3. a	4. c	5. b	6. b	7. a	8. c	9. a	10. a
13B	1. C, D, O	2. F, F, O	3. 2, 3, 1	4. C, C, F	5. B, M, N					

14A	1. a	2. a	3. a	4. c	5. b	6. c	7. a	8. b	9. b	10. a
14B	1. C, O, D		2. O, F, F		3. 1, 2, 3		4. F, C, C		5. B, M, N	
15A	1. b	2. a	3. b	4. a	5. b	6. b	7. c	8. a	9. a	10. b
15B	1. C, D, O		2. F, F, O		3. 3, 2, 1		4. C, C, F		5. B, M, N	
16A	1. b	2. a	3. c	4. b	5. a	6. a	7. c	8. c	9. a	10. a
16B	1. C, O, D		2. F, F, O		3. 2, 1, 3		4. F, C, C		5. N, M, B	
17A	1. c	2. b	3. c	4. a	5. b	6. c	7. b	8. c	9. a	10. a
17B	1. O, C, D		2. O, F, F,		3. 3, 1, 2		4. F, C, C		5. N, M, B	
18A	1. a	2. a	3. b	4. c	5. b	6. b	7. c	8. a	9. a	10. c
18b	1. O, C, D		2. F, O, F		3. 2, 1, 3		4. C, F, C		5. N, M, B	
19A	1. c	2. b	3. a	4. b	5. c	6. a	7. c	8. a	9. c	10. a
19B	1. C, O, D		2. F, F, O		3. 3, 1, 2		4. C, C, F		5. N, M, B	
20A	1. a	2. a	3. b	4. b	5. c	6. a	7. a	8. c	9. a	10. c
20B	1. D, O, C		2. F, F, O		3. 3, 2, 1		4. C, C, F		5. B, M, N	
21A	1. a	2. a	3. c	4. b	5. c	6. a	7. b	8. a	9. c	10. b
21B	1. O, C, D		2. F, O, F		3. 1, 3, 2		4. F, C, C		5. M, B, N	
22A	1. b	2. b	3. c	4. a	5. b	6. a	7. c	8. b	9. a	10. c
22b	1. O, C, D		2. F, O, F		3. 1, 2, 3		4. C, F, C		5. M, N, B	
23A	1. a	2. a	3. b	4. a	5. b	6. a	7. c	8. c	9. a	10. b
23B	1. C, O, D		2. F, F, O		3. 1, 3, 2		4. F, C, C		5. M, N, B	
24A	1. b	2. c	3. a	4. c	5. b	6. a	7. c	8. a	9. b	10. b
24b	1. C, D, O		2. F, F, O		3. 3, 2, 1		4. C, F, C		5. M, N, B	
25A	1. b	2. a	3. c	4. c	5. b	6. b	7. b	8. a	9. b	10. b
25B	1. O, C, D		2. F, F, O		3. 3, 1, 2		4. C, F, C		5. M, N, B	

READING RATE

Put an X on the line above each lesson number to show your reading time and words-per-minute rate for that lesson.

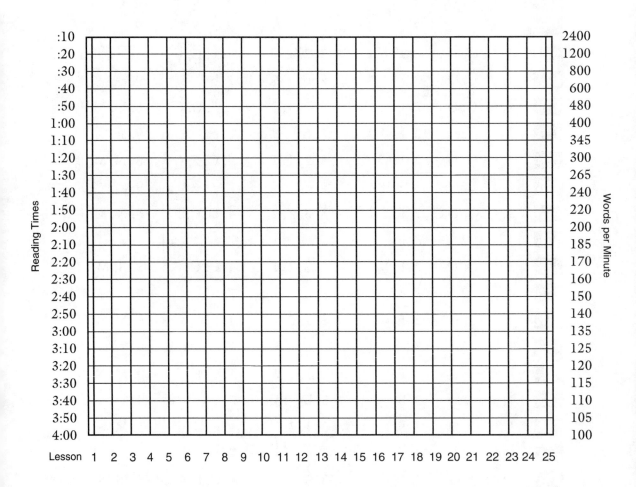

COMPREHENSION SCORE

Put an X on the line above each lesson number to indicate your total correct answers and comprehension score for that lesson.

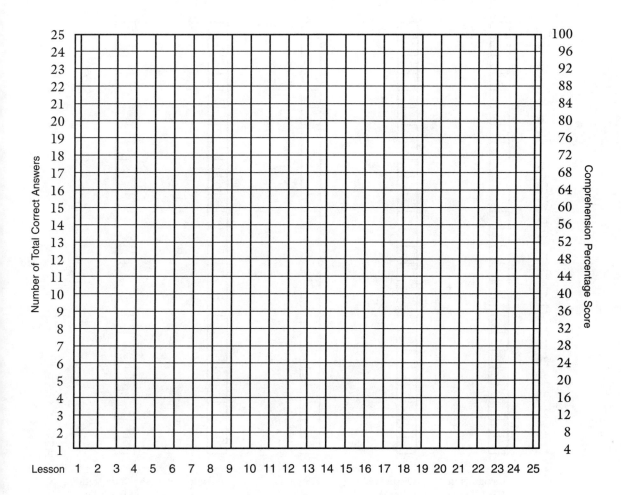

COMPREHENSION SKILLS PROFILE

Put an X in the box above each question type to indicate an incorrect response to any question of that type.

	Recognizing Words in Context	Distinguishing Fact from Opinion	Keeping Events in Order	Making Correct Inferences	Understanding Main Ideas
Lesson 1					
2					
3					
4					
5					
6					
7					
8					
9					
10					
11					
12					
13					
14					
15					
16					
17					
18					
19					
20					
21					
22					
23					
24					
25					